Creative Plastics
Techniques

Claude Smale

Creative Plastics Techniques

Claude Smale

Van Nostrand Reinhold Company Regional Offices:
New York   Cincinnati   Chicago   Millbrae   Dallas
Van Nostrand Reinhold Company International Offices:
London   Toronto   Melbourne

Library of Congress Catalogue Card Number 75-3988
ISBN 0 442 29952 4

Designed by Rod Josey; printed in Great Britain
by Jolly and Barber Ltd., Rugby; and bound by the
Ferndale Book Company.

Published by Van Nostrand Company Inc., 450 West 33rd Street
New York, N.Y. 10001 and Van Nostrand Company Ltd., 25-28
Buckingham Gate, London SW1E 6LQ

Published simultaneously in Canada by Van Nostrand Reinhold
Company Ltd.

16 15 14 13 12 11 10 9 8 7 6 5 4 3 2 1

Contents

Introduction

PLASTICS AND SOCIETY

The plastics industry has come into its own in the lifetime of many of us and, even now, the annual growth rate is over 10 per cent. By the 1980s, it is reliably predicted, the world consumption of plastics by volume will exceed that of all metals, and this trend seems destined to continue since the traditional materials, which mainly come from natural sources, are in some cases in short supply and in others expensive to produce. As the price of commodities in traditional materials has risen higher and higher, the cost of plastics has remained fairly constant — which, effectively, means they have become cheaper.

Until recently, they were in no way essential in our daily lives; for years man got on perfectly well without them, but in a short space of time they have become crucial to our civilization. At the moment the benefits far outweigh the few disadvantages but, bearing in mind the truly immense volume of material the world will shortly consume, it is of prime importance that plastics should be properly used. Production on such a scale is bound to present hazards, and these must be anticipated and allowed for if the benefits to our lives are not to be affected adversely.

Most of us have not noticed the rate at which our consumption of plastics has increased and it is surprising perhaps that it has increased so dramatically when, in fact, there is still some resistance to their complete acceptance.

TOWARDS AN AESTHETIC

Many people do not find plastics materials attractive; they may even have a positive revulsion for waxy textured materials like polythene. Acrylics seem to be more readily accepted but, even so, not perhaps with the same assurance as traditional naturally occurring materials. Perhaps this is because it is not possible to relate plastics to a known source or raw material with which people are familiar. They know that wool comes from sheep and wood from trees, but plastics — they have just arrived! For a long time also, the term 'plastic' was synonymous with goods that were cheap or imitative of products made in other materials: there was the 'real' thing and 'plastic' was a cheap substitute. The industry is well aware that a stigma still attaches to the word but, as more and more well-designed goods find their way on to the market, plastics are increasingly accepted and understood as materials in their own right.

It seems, nevertheless, that there is something about the very quality of plastics that people find disagreeable. When assessed from the visual or tactile aspects alongside the traditional materials, the preference is invariably for the latter. Yet there is nothing inherently wrong with plastics as a group of materials; although they are produced artificially, they have their own integrity and their practical advantages must be beyond dispute. So are we right even to consider plastics in the same light as the traditional materials, or to look for aesthetic qualities in the visual/tactile sense? Have we been so conditioned in our responses to natural materials that we cannot make the necessary adjustments for plastics or must we seek new criteria? Even men of good taste are at variance with each other. There is no doubt that we are still 'feeling our way', and until we have established our criteria, we shall find their complete acceptance difficult and be in doubt about our attitude towards them.

PLASTICS AND EDUCATION

Our inability to come to terms with many of the problems posed by plastics stems, in part at least, from basic ignorance. The man in the street, the consumer, knows little about plastics; it would be unusual indeed to find a layman who could say why his ball-point pen softened under heat when his ash-tray did not, but it would not be unusual if the same man had a very passable knowledge of woods and metals. It all depends on previous experience. Most of us, at some time or other, have worked with traditional materials, if only at school, and this experience helped our appreciation of their basic properties. But few of us were ever introduced to plastics and, now that we use plastics to such an extent, they should surely be included in the school syllabus. This is bound to be a slow process for, before this can come about, teachers themselves have to be taught and, most important, shown that projects in plastics are within their capabilities and can be carried out with school equipment.

CAN PLASTICS BE A CRAFT SUBJECT?

It is an essential characteristic of plastics that they lend themselves admirably to mass-production processes: their moulding is simple, they reproduce accurately, they can be self-coloured and need no finishing. Also, unlike industries using clay, wood or metal, little of the industry can be said to be 'craft based'; there are few hand operations involving the plastics material itself. By comparison, traditional industries are not 'mechanized' in the same way; it is seldom possible to put raw material into one end of a machine and obtain the finished product at the other. More often than not, they retain traditional skills which have become mechanically assisted.

Because the main bulk of plastics materials produced is taken up by the mass-producing industry, the materials manufacturers, not unnaturally, formulate their products to meet the needs of mass-production. They are produced to an accurate specification with flawless but mainly uninteresting surfaces and, except when he mixes the materials himself, as in the case of polyesters, the craftsman has limited control over their make up.

From this it might be inferred that plastics are essentially mass-producing materials and that the traditional materials are more suited to craft-type activities. This is essentially true; nevertheless there does exist a remarkable range of legitimate 'craft' techniques for forming the range of plastics which are not made as moulding powders. These can be worked with methods which involve handwork and considerable skills. Also, many of the 'industrial' techniques can be carried out with simplified machines and, while the operation of the machine itself does not require much skill, the preparation of the moulds, formers, dies etc. requires very considerable skills — even though these usually involve traditional materials. It would seem that a high degree of craftsmanship is called for in 'industrial' plastics, but it is not craftsmanship in the usual sense of the word; plastics are not generally worked by individual craftsmen in the traditional manner with a hallowed regard for the qualities of the material, though there are several plastics whose qualities can be exploited in this way.

HOW MUCH IS IT NECESSARY TO KNOW?

To the layman, the world of plastics must be quite confusing, for there is an immense variety of plastics possessing many different properties. Each one is different from the other because of some peculiarity in its chemical or physical make-up. These chemical differences may be quite obscure to the layman, and even the names themselves are hard to grasp for they in no way hint at distinguishing characteristics. Typically, Perspex or Plexiglas is 'polymethyl methacrylate', ABS is 'acrylonitrile butadiene styrene'. Hard words to learn and, to complicate the matter further, certain brand names have become commonly used to describe generic types, e.g., Bakelite for phenolic resins.

The working properties of the materials used in the traditional industries tend to remain constant. Any newcomer can readily get some grasp of them if he works with them for a short period. A craftsman gains an 'understanding' of his materials by an intuitive feel for their inherent characteristics. It is true that individual plastics can be worked with no more than this kind of natural feeling for materials, but it is unlikely in itself to be sufficient for general work in the plastics field. Indeed, anyone who attempts this without some better knowledge is likely to be seriously misled, for the fact that a plastic may possess a certain tactile quality of working in one set of circumstances is no indication that it will retain it in different conditions. In any case, plastics do not have a single set of working characteristics; to a great extent, manufacturers can vary their properties at will to match whatever is wanted. To understand plastics properly, therefore, something more than a feeling for materials is required; it is necessary to know a little about *how* and *why* the various types differ and behave as they do.

HEALTH AND SAFETY

There are health and safety hazards connected with the processing of most materials and, if handled indiscriminately, plastics are no exception. While the dangers are probably no greater than with traditional materials, the worker should take simple precautions to avoid inhalation of fumes or skin contact where necessary. The following recommendations apply generally:

1. Certain monomers, cements, volatile solvents or plastics vapours may be narcotic in action, causing irritation to the eyes, drowsiness, stomach upset or skin disorder. Whenever they are used, or where plastics is likely to be heated, it is essential always to ensure that there is *adequate ventilation*.

2. Repeated handling of solvents may cause the skin to become over sensitive and easily aggravated by more harmful substances. *Barrier creams* are recommended.

3. Smoking should not be permitted and, while many plastics are made in self-extinguishing grades, normal *fire precautions* should be observed. Many of the additives, solvents, peroxides and catalysts are highly inflammable and can cause spontaneous combustion if stored together. These should always be isolated both for storage and for waste disposal.

4. Always *follow the manufacturers' instructions*.

5. Notes on safety are available from the Plastics Institute.

PART 1
THE NATURE
OF PLASTICS

Chapter 1
Some Basic
Facts

THE BEGINNINGS

Horn, shellac, gutta percha and amber are all naturally occurring plastics materials and man has made use of them since primeval times. Man-made plastics as we know them today are very much synthetic materials made possible by man's knowledge of chemistry. As the study of chemistry itself is a comparatively recent phenomenon, it is only in the last hundred years or so that plastics have been known and most materials were developed in the last fifty years.

As a result of the discovery of the reaction between nitric acid and cotton, explosives were developed — and, indirectly, cellulosic plastics. In the 1860s, an Englishman called Alexander Parkes produced commercially a new material he had invented called Parkesine. This was basically a cellulose nitrate and from it he produced a range of decorative goods and trinkets. Although he had in this material the basis of Celluloid, Parkes's business did not succeed and it was the Americans who developed the material commercially. Celluloid became essential to the growing cinematograph industry and there were various derivatives; dope for the aircraft industry and rayon, for example. The main drawback with cellulose nitrate was its inflammability, but later variations of cellulose plastics were much improved in this respect.

At first, man was attempting to find substitutes for the natural plastics: Celluloid was developed as a substitute for ivory, Bakelite was discovered as a result of researches for a substitute for shellac. Bakelite, a phenol formaldehyde resin, was the first plastics moulding material and it is still used today. It became so common that its name became synonymous with moulded plastics goods. Other plastics which are now commonplace were only developed following extensive scientific research.

During the 1930s PVC, polystyrene and acrylics were produced in fair quantities and nylon was developed in America. Later, polythene was developed in Great Britain. Today, plastics are produced with a wide range of properties and it is possible to select a grade for almost any application. Often, if the demands are stringent, the manufacturer can produce a special grade to match them. It is perhaps the distinctive ability of the plastics industry to adapt its basic materials in this way that contributes to its versatility and extraordinary rate of growth.

RAW MATERIALS

The commonest raw materials are coal, petroleum, plants and milk. Cellulosic plastics are made from the cellulose in plants such as cotton which have a high cellulose content. Milk provides casein which is the basis of another group of plastics, but by far the greatest bulk of plastics is derived from coal and oil. Organic compounds are carbon based and it is well known that coal and oil are the decomposed remains of vegetation which grew upon the earth in primeval times. The carbon basis of the original material remains, even though its chemistry may be altered by decomposition processes. When raw materials are adapted into plastics materials, in some cases the basic extracts have to undergo further chemical treatment, in others they are just purified.

CARBON STRUCTURES

Atoms can be considered to have 'arms' with which they link with other atoms, the number of arms varying from one atom to another. Hydrogen has one arm, oxygen has two arms and carbon has four arms. Because it has four arms, the carbon atom is capable of linking in a wide variety of ways, forming chains, rings and networks. In fact, carbon atoms can link, or in the chemist's terms 'bond', to form a greater variety of compounds than all other atoms put together. Thus there is an immense range of carbon based materials (including all living matter) and plastics are a sub-group of these. There is a strong inclination for carbon atoms to link with hydrogen, oxygen and nitrogen, and when they link with these, or with chlorine or fluorine, plastics materials may be produced.

Most of the carbon compounds derived from oil have carbon molecules joined in 'chains', and most of those obtained from coal-tar have carbon molecules joined in 'rings'. The simplest carbon ring compound is benzene. From crude oil is derived a family of carbon and hydrogen-based compounds known as the 'paraffins'. The word paraffin means inactive, and since the paraffins do not participate in chemical reactions other than burning, the name is appropriate. The simplest member of the paraffin family is an odourless, colourless gas known as 'methane' which has a simple molecule comprising one carbon atom and four hydrogen atoms.*

*Element: any substance which cannot be divided into simpler substances.
Compound: two or more elements in chemical combination.
Atom: the smallest part of an element which is capable of reacting chemically.
Molecule: the smallest part of an element or compound which can exist separately.

Diagram 1 illustrates the structure of simple paraffins. Notice how each successive member contains one carbon atom and two hydrogen atoms more than the previous member. Notice also that each carbon atom is linked by *single* bonds. Compounds with such a single bonded structure are known as 'saturated' compounds. If the carbon atoms in a material are *double* bonded to other atoms, the material is known as 'unsaturated'. Ethylene is a typical unsaturated compound.

DIAGRAM 1. ALKANES

METHANE CH_4

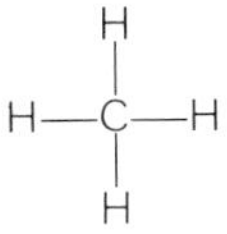

ETHANE C_2H_6

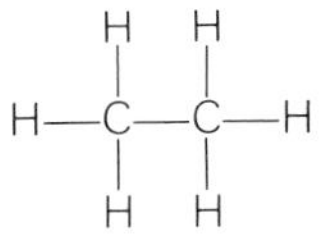

PROPANE C_3H_8

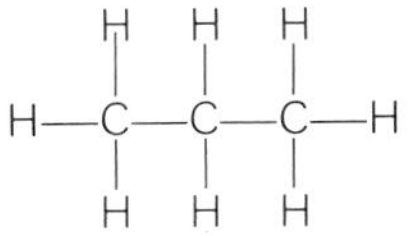

BUTANE C_4H_{10}

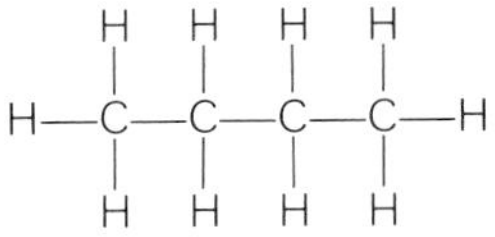

POLYMERIZATION

In Diagram 2a, representing the molecule of ethylene, notice that the carbon atoms are double bonded leaving only four arms to take hydrogen atoms.

It is a fact that when double bonds exist, one of them can easily be broken and the arms so released caused to join up with corresponding arms from like structures. In this way, long chain molecules can be produced. This process is known as an 'addition polymerization'; Diagram 2b illustrates how the double bond of ethylene is adapted to form the chain-like structure of polyethylene. Polyethylene is the chemical name for polythene.

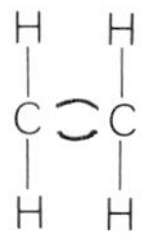

ETHYLENE C₂H₄
(Monomer) DIAGRAM 2a.

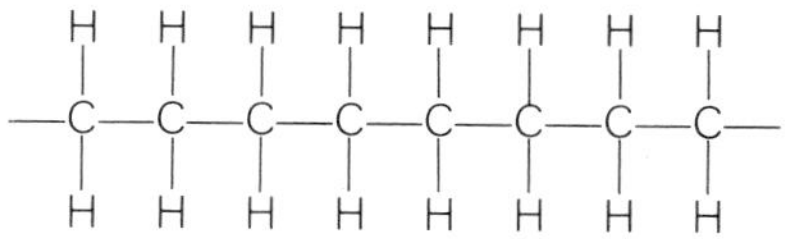

POLYETHYLENE
(Polymer) DIAGRAM 2b.

Notice that the ethylene is called a 'monomer' and that polyethylene is called a 'polymer'. Basic units such as ethylene, which have the ability to form chains in this way, are called monomers. Some monomers are liquids, some are gases. A polymer is a number of such monomer units joined in a chain. Whenever the word 'poly' precedes the name of a substance, it describes a long chain molecule of that substance. A 'high polymer' is the name given to a particularly long-chained substance.

'Polymerization' is the name given to the process of building up molecular chains. When the molecules react additively in the way described for ethylene, the process is known as 'addition polymerization'. There is another method of polymerization known as 'condensation polymerization' which usually involves two different monomers. At least one of the monomers possesses molecules containing two or more reactive groups of atoms and the other monomer may possess molecules containing one or more reactive groups. When these monomers interact chemically, plastics materials are produced which may have either a cross-linked or a linear system of bonding. The process differs from addition polymerization in that simple by-products such as water or hydrogen chloride are eliminated – hence the term 'condensation'. As an example, urea and formaldehyde produce UF resin (Diagram 3).

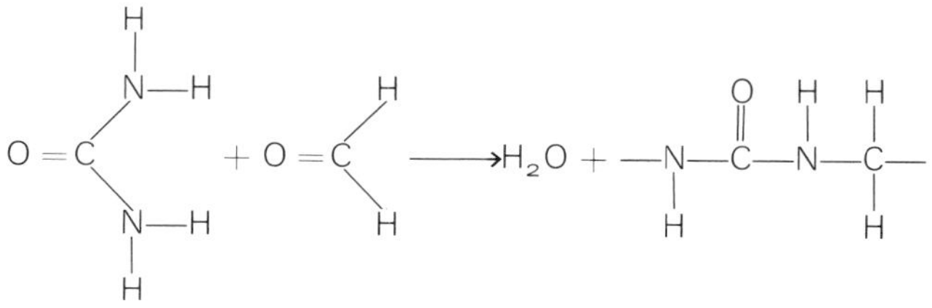

UREA
DIAGRAM 3.

FORMALDE-HYDE

UREA-FORMALDE-HYDE RESIN

Sometimes different kinds of monomers are joined together in a chain to obtain special characteristics not found in either of their normal polymers. This process is known as 'co-polymerization' and the products are 'co-polymers'. Vinyl chloride/vinyl acetate co-polymer is perhaps the most common. It possesses the toughness of polyvinyl chloride with the heat stability of polyvinyl acetate.

CHEMICAL MODIFICATION OF POLYMERS TO PRODUCE PLASTICS WITH DIFFERENT PROPERTIES

The replacement of some of the hydrogen atoms in the ethylene molecule by other atoms or groups of atoms produces a variety of monomers which have a common backbone and therefore belong to the same family. Diagram 4 shows how different monomers can be achieved and how they can be linked into chains. Notice how, for example, a chlorine atom produces PVC (polyvinyl chloride) or a benzene ring produces polystyrene. Although these two materials have a common spine, their properties are very different indeed.

CHAIN AND CROSS-LINKED STRUCTURES
(Diagram 5)

Long chain molecular structures are a distinctive characteristic of plastics and rubbers. The molecules of plastics are generally exceptionally large compared with other substances but, even though the number of atoms in some high polymers may run into thousands, the largest molecule would not measure beyond .001" in length. 'Thermoplastic' materials are built up of long-chain molecules which exist like separate threads, intermingled in a complex but mostly random fashion. Each and every thread or chain is linked with its neighbour by weak intermolecular forces. These are known as van der Waals forces and are much weaker than the chemical bonds of the atoms making up the chains. Heating can cause some breakdown of the forces between the chains: the molecules 'vibrate' with the result that they may be parted from each other fairly easily. Thus they are free to slide over each other, but as soon as the heating is removed, the intermolecular forces become reassertive and the molecules are again transfixed. The sliding molecules lend the quality of plasticity. This characteristic is possessed by all 'thermoplastic' materials: when subjected to heat they soften and when cooled they return to a rigid state.

'Thermosetting' plastics, however, have a system of cross linking between the chains which produces a giant three-dimensional network structure which is completely rigid. Thus thermosetting plastics do not possess the

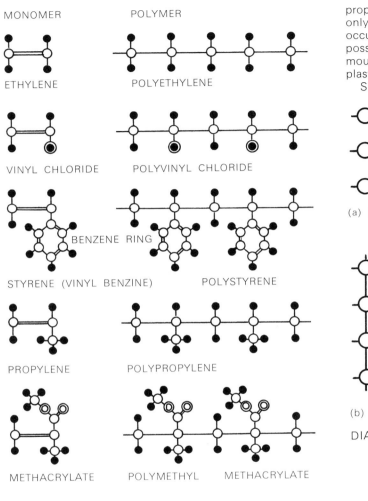

MONOMER | POLYMER

ETHYLENE | POLYETHYLENE

VINYL CHLORIDE | POLYVINYL CHLORIDE

BENZENE RING

STYRENE (VINYL BENZINE) | POLYSTYRENE

PROPYLENE | POLYPROPYLENE

METHACRYLATE | POLYMETHYL METHACRYLATE

○ CARBON ● HYDROGEN ◉ OXYGEN ● CHLORINE

DIAGRAM 4. SOME ADDITION POLYMERS,
THE VINYLS

property of softening when reheated; they are heated once only during the manufacturing process and the cross linking occurs at this time. When first heated they soften and possess temporary plasticity which allows them to be moulded, but once they have set hard, they cannot be made plastic again.

Some materials do not strictly fit into either category.

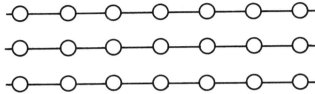

(a) LINEAR CHAIN THERMOPLASTICS

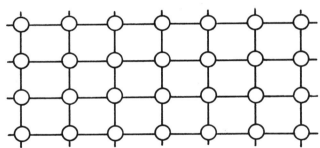

(b) CROSS-LINKING OF THERMOSETTING PLASTICS

DIAGRAM 5.

Chapter 2
The Properties of Plastics

We saw in Chapter I that plastics materials can be divided into two main groups: 'thermoplastic' and 'thermosetting'. 'Thermoplastic' materials have the property of softening under the application of moderate heat and becoming rigid again on cooling — normally at room temperatures. When a thermoplastic material is heated to working temperature, no significant chemical change takes place, so that the material will resoften if it is reheated. The cycle can be repeated many times. 'Thermosetting' materials, on the other hand, can be heat treated once only. Under the initial application of heat they become soft but, when this heating is sustained, a chemical change takes place and the material sets hard. This rigid state is completely permanent and nothing can cause the material to revert to the plastic state. Sustained overheating only leads to degradation of the material.

ADJUSTING THE PROPERTIES OF PLASTICS
We also saw in Chapter I how the basic polymers were built up, but these basic polymers cannot be used for fabricating or moulding purposes without further modification.

Plasticizers These are added to the plastics in the original mix to lower their softening temperatures and to make them less brittle. Cellulosic plastics and PVC (polyvinyl chloride), for example, are very hard in the original state and have softening temperatures too high for ease of working. By controlling the amount of plasticizer incorporated, however, chemists can alter the physical qualities of the material from very hard to soft and flabby. Soft PVC rainwear and rigid rain-water goods illustrate how plasticizers can affect the properties of a common basic material. The chemical effect of the plasticizer is to come between the molecules of the polymer causing some release of their normal bonds. The effect is similar to heating; the molecules are more free to slide past each other and so plasticity is increased. If large quantities of plasticizer are added, the molecules become very dispersed and the material becomes liquid.

In this way, some adhesives and paints are prepared.
Lubricants These are substances which have a lubricating effect in the processing, making the material more 'fatty' in texture so that it flows easily.
Catalysts The formation of a polymer by the assembly of molecules is a form of chemical reaction. A catalyst is a material which affects the speed of a reaction without itself undergoing change. Normally a catalyst speeds up a reaction, but a material which retards a reaction is known as a 'negative catalyst'. An 'inhibitor' is a substance which hinders the effect of a catalyst.
Pigments Materials are generally transparent, opaque or translucent. Mostly they are easily coloured and, when pigments are included in the mix, the resultant plastics is coloured all the way through and may not require subsequent finishing.
Fillers Fillers are inert powders which are added to polymers. Typical of those employed are wood flour, asbestos and cotton; wood flour and cotton improve the impact strength and asbestos enhances heat resistance. Sometimes fillers are used simply to economise on the more expensive polymer and, when used in this way, they are known as 'extenders'.

Fillers very much affect the working characteristics of a material; some operations which are quite feasible with the unfilled material become quite impossible when fillers are added.
Stabilizers These are included to protect the material against deterioration and are of two types: heat stabilizers, which enable the material to resist degradation during processing, and those which help resistance to the ultra-violet rays in sunlight.
Antioxidants These resist deterioration due to oxidation either in processing or in subsequent use.
Solvents Solvents affect plastics in much the same way as heat; they cause the electro-static charges between molecules to weaken so that the molecules can move freely across each other. The cross-linked structure of thermosetting plastics is less easily disturbed, so that these materials are highly resistant to solvents. (See Table 6.)

THE RESPONSE OF PLASTICS TO HEATING
In all operations involving thermoplastics, two important factors must be taken into account.
    (a) That the heat capacity of all plastics is high.
    (b) That the thermal conductivity of all plastics is low.
Since these two factors govern the rate of heating and cooling, they effectively determine the rate of production.
    Diagram 6 illustrates how slowly heat is transferred in

plastics compared with metals, and this low thermal conductivity is a fundamental problem in processing. Heat applied to the outside face of a sheet, for example, takes a considerable time to penetrate to the inside.

DIAGRAM 6.
Time to conduct one calorie of heat through one cubic centimetre of material with a temperature difference of one centigrade degree.

	HOURS	MINUTES	SECONDS
WOOD	4	10	
POLYPROPYLENE	1	18	
PVC	1	1	
ASBESTOS		35	
NYLON		32	
POLYTHENE		28	
STEEL			9
BRASS/ZINC			4
ALUMINIUM			2
COPPER			1

Data by courtesy of Mr J. Bown

Some plastics, particularly PVC (polyvinyl chloride), are sensitive to heat and need careful handling even at their normal working temperatures.

When taken to higher temperatures, molten plastics generally retain high viscosity; they do not become runny like most metals.

Plastics also expand and contract with temperature changes to a much greater extent than do metals, though this may be governed by the nature of filler included. When cooling from the plastic state to room temperature, typical percentages of volume contraction are shown in Diagram 7.

On average, plastics have rates of thermal expansion eight times as high as metals, and these discrepancies must be accommodated in the design of moulds.

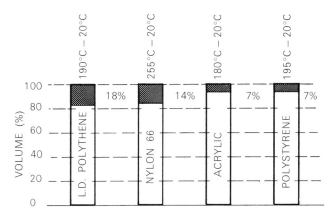

DIAGRAM 7. VOLUME CONTRACTION ON COOLING
Data by courtesy of Mr. J. Bown

THE RESPONSE OF PLASTICS TO STRESS

Stretch and yield The molecules in rubber take up a random or amorphous arrangement possessing weak intermolecular forces. When the material is stretched, the molecules become increasingly aligned in the direction of the force. When the force is released, they revert to their original arrangement so that the material recovers its shape. Thermoplastics exhibit less elasticity because their molecular structure is partly amorphous and partly crystalline. In crystalline areas, the molecules are already aligned. Also, the intermolecular forces are stronger than in rubber. Thermosetting plastics, because of the cross-linking already described, are rigid.

When a piece of PVC is stretched, the molecules move over each other and, so long as the stretching force is not greater than the intermolecular forces, the latter will cause the material to revert to its original shape as soon as the load is removed. When, however, the applied force begins to exceed the cohesional forces between the chains, more and more molecules may be displaced with respect to each other and, as the material lengthens and the section thins, little or no increase of force is required to extend it further.

The 'yield' point of a plastic generally describes the load and the conditions under which the molecules begin to flow under stress, and it is markedly affected by time and temperature. This can be demonstrated by stretching a strip of thermoplastic film, first at ambient temperature and then when it is warmed. Generally, plastics become more brittle the more the temperature is lowered but the transition in physical properties may take place over a broad or a narrow range of temperatures.

Molecular orientation The mechanical strength of a material is very much affected by its molecular arrangement. If a filament of nylon is stretched, the molecules become separated and realigned in the direction of pull. The effect is not dissimilar to drawing out a thread of wool, the molecules corresponding to the wool fibres. This allows strong bonds to develop between the parallel molecules, and for this reason drawn fibres actually *gain* in strength.

Manufacturing processes induce similar strains; when molten material is made to flow through a constricted opening, the long molecules tend to become aligned in the direction of flow. Where such orientation exists, it is far easier to break the piece along the line of orientation than across it and this effect is made use of in the polypropylene hinge.

Polythene, because it is flexible, is able to withstand impacts that would shatter polystyrene. This is because the molecules of polythene are able to move more easily than the molecules of polystyrene. Polystyrene, it will be remembered, has large benzene rings attached to its carbon spine and these tend to interlock. The immobility of the molecules makes the material brittle. Relative impact strengths are given in Table 10.

WEATHERING
Sunlight contains ultra-violet rays and plastics are able to resist these to a variety of degrees as shown in Table 7. Acrylics (Perspex, Plexiglas) seem more or less unaffected, but on the other end of the scale some polystyrenes are badly affected in a few months. To counteract degradation, manufacturers include additives in special grades of plastics. Carbon black, because it is an excellent absorber of ultra-violet light, is frequently incorporated and can extend the life of plastics twenty or thirty times.

THE ADVANTAGES AND DISADVANTAGES OF PLASTICS
Modern plastics compare favourably with traditional materials for many applications. Only the heavy metals exhibit properties which are totally beyond them.

ADVANTAGES
Colour Compared with other materials, a wide colour range is available with varying degrees of opacity and transparency. Plastics also have the advantage that they are coloured all the way through.

Strength with light weight Weight for weight, plastics are stronger than steel and they are also comparatively resilient. Their impact strength in the flexible grades is so good that they are almost indestructible in normal usage.

Electrical insulation Most plastics are excellent insulators and this factor has been significant in the electrical industry. Their low rate of water absorption also helps in this respect.

Thermal insulation The low thermal conductivity of plastics has already been described, and it is to be expected that they perform well as heat insulators.

Durability The high resistance to chemical attack can be seen in Table 6. Plastics are generally more resistant to corrosion than metals.

Moulding properties Moulded articles generally reproduce accurately the contours of the mould and require little finishing.

DISADVANTAGES
Heat degradation Although some heat-resistant types are available, the majority of plastics cannot be used in situations where higher temperatures are involved. As plastics consist mainly of carbon atoms, this is perhaps not unexpected. Over 150°C most plastics are affected. All plastics burn in certain conditions though they may be formulated in such a way that they do not burn in normal circumstances.

Creep Plastics creep or deflect under a constant load. Even though they sometimes recover when the load is removed, this is a serious hindrance to their use in structural applications.

Surface hardness Plastics generally do not exhibit a high degree of surface hardness. The hardest, such as acrylics (Perspex, Plexiglas) correspond to aluminium. On the other hand, resistance to abrasion, e.g. nylon used in mechanical assemblies, can be better than metals.

Static electricity Plastics are prone to develop electro-static charges, with the result that dust particles cling to the surface.

Chapter 3
Some Important Plastics

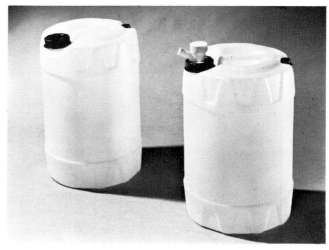

Typical containers in polyethylene made from BP Chemicals Rigidex polythene material.

THE FAMILIES OF PLASTICS
THERMOSOFTENING
Vinyls

Polythene (high density)	Polypropylene
Polythene (low density)	PTFE
Polystyrene	(polytetrafluoroethylene)

ABS (acrylonitrile butadiene styrene)	Acrylic (polymethyl methacrylate)
PVC (polyvinyl chloride) Rigid	
PVC (polyvinyl chloride) Flexible	

Cellulosics

Cellulose acetate	Cellulose nitrate
CAB (cellulose acetate butyrate)	

Polyamides
Nylons

THERMOHARDENING

Phenolics
PF (phenol formaldehyde) resins

Epoxides
Epoxy resins

Aminos
UF (urea formaldehyde) resins
MF (melamine formaldehyde) resins

Alkyds
Polyesters

Polyethylene Polyethylene is commonly known in its contracted form as polythene. In the raw state, it is a rigid, whitish, translucent material which is modified to produce two basic types — High Density and Low Density. These may be referred to as HD polythene or LD polythene, or as LDPE or HDPE. In fact, the difference in densities is small but their properties are very different.

HDPE is invariably stiffer than LDPE and has an appreciably higher softening temperature which enables it to be used for such applications as sterilizing. It is also more transparent.

LDPE has a greasy texture and is more or less chemically inert. It is easily worked at relatively low temperatures and makes up into articles which are extremely durable and tough. A high proportion of LD polythene is made into film.

Special characteristics:
self coloured	tough
resistant to chemicals	outstanding electrical
can remain flexible over a wide temp. range	insulator
	can be made clear

Applications:
toys, LD, HD	pipes for plumbing and cold water supply, HD
domestic utensils, LD, HD	
electric wire insulation LD	sacks, LD
industrial/chemical containers, LD, HD	heavy duty film for building/agriculture, LD
domestic bottles and containers, LD, HD	packaging film, LD

Polypropylene Polypropylene is not unlike HD polythene, but it has a higher surface hardness and is more glossy. It has the lowest density of all thermoplastics in common use, thus a larger volume of goods can be produced from a given weight of material. Its melting point is significantly higher

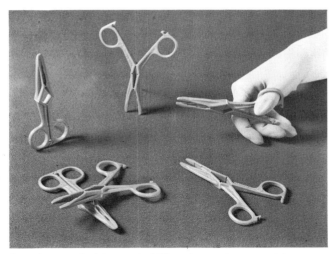

One piece medical forceps in ICI's polypropylene material Propathene, demonstrating an excellent use of the integral hinge. Marketed by the Medical Aids Dept. of ICI's Pharmaceuticals Division.

than that of polythene, and compared with LD polythene it has high tensile strength. It would normally be selected before polythene only when its special characteristics can be utilized. Perhaps its outstanding property is that of flexing without fatigue, due to molecular orientation — a property commonly exploited in integral hinges. Poly-propylene materials are produced as pure polymers of propylene or as co-polymers of propylene and ethylene.

Special characteristics:

light weight	can withstand constant
tough	flexing
resistant to chemicals	hard glossy surface
	can be self coloured

Main applications:

domestic goods	toys
sterilizing equipment	plumbing fittings/piping
self-hinged containers	films
yarns, ropes	crates

PTFE (polytetrafluoroethylene) As PTFE is expensive to produce, its use is restricted. Its outstanding characteristic is its low coefficient of friction—so low that it approxi-

Right: Decorative screen made of cut and folded polypropylene sheet. The opaque areas at the folds are due to stresses in the sheet.

mates to that of ice. In addition, it can withstand relatively high temperatures and is very resistant to chemical attack. It cannot be injection moulded, because even when melted it has high viscosity. Mouldings are produced by a process called sintering: powder is packed into a mould which is heated to the point at which the particles coalesce. It is produced commercially as (a) dispersions for surface coating or impregnation, (b) powders for inclusion in greases and lubricants, (c) extrusions, or (d) powders for moulding.

PVC (polyvinyl chloride) More PVC is produced than any other plastics material. In pure polymer form it cannot be worked; it is too hard and has too high a softening temperature. It is only the addition of plasticizers which enables it to be processed. Some materials contain a high proportion of plasticizer; these are flexible and have a low softening temperature. Those with less plasticizer are more rigid, and are sometimes known as 'unplasticized' or UPVC. The material is produced as extrusions, films, granules and pastes (plastisols).

Special characteristics:
  corrosion resistance   wide range of
  good electrical insulator   flexibilities/hardnesses
  good abrasion resistance   toughness
                              easy to process

Applications:
  extrusions (pipes/plumbing fittings, packaging
    sachets, cable insulation, rain-water goods)
  films (packaging, agriculture, inflatable goods, rain-
    wear)
  mouldings (containers, domestic goods, electrical
    fittings)

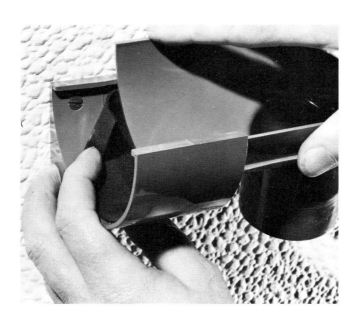

Opposite page bottom left: Rainwater goods made in Breon PVC by Allied Structural Plastics, Ltd. *Photo: BP Chemicals.*

Opposite page top: Travelling cases made from Storeys Moonglow material which is based on BP Chemicals Breon PVC.

Opposite page bottom right: Clock case made in flexible PVC by Jane Wheeler, 1st year student. *Photo: West Surrey College of Art and Design.*

Left: The transparency of acrylic is well displayed in this fitting for the display of jewellery. Made in Perspex. *Photo: ICI Plastics Division.*

The optical effects obtainable with acrylic materials are well utilized in these photographs. Below: *Relief Plexiglas* by Le Parc; Overleaf: *Déplacement optique* by Boto. *Photos: Galerie Denise René, Paris.*

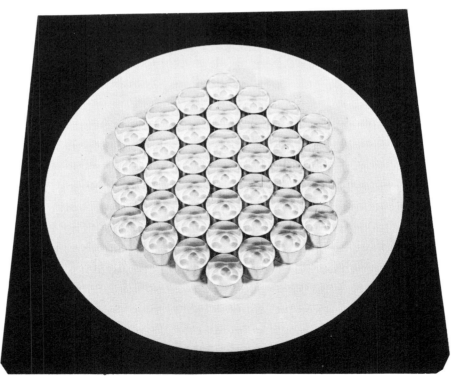

sheet (flooring, leathercloth)
coatings (wallpapers, fabrics, metal coating)

Acrylics Acrylics are chemically known as polymethyl methacrylate or PMMA. Perspex and Plexiglas are well known trade names. Its light-transmission properties are better than most glasses and it is made in a variety of block, sheet, and extruded forms. Because of its transparency and reflective characteristics, it is capable of 'piping' light around corners; a rod bent to a complex form will transmit a high proportion of light from one end to the other. For the same reasons, the edges appear luminous in transparent grades and the effect is made use of in display work.

Special characteristics:

high clarity/surface finish	excellent weathering
hard surface	characteristics
good machining qualities	comparatively light
	weight

Applications:

light fittings	display work/signs etc.
aircraft canopies	domestic/sanitary ware
can be used as a castable	
material for embedding	

Polystyrene Sometimes known as PS, polystyrene is produced in sheet form for thermoforming, in granular form for moulding, and in various expanded grades known as EPS. Because it is cheap, easy to produce and flows easily when molten, it is universally used for injection mouldings which will not be subjected to great stress. In clear form, it can be highly transparent, passing about 90 per cent of visible light. It is also sold in toughened form (modified with synthetic rubber) which is used a great deal in preformed disposable packaging. Its weakness in the normal form is its brittleness. Such grades are so brittle as to produce a metallic ring when struck.

Special characteristics:

outstanding flow	easily manufactured
properties when heated	low cost
rigidity	brittle unless toughened
easily coloured in a	
wide range	

Applications:

general purpose consumer	in expanded grades is
goods	used for building
toys	insulation, packaging
components and	inserts etc.
accessories of many	electrical mouldings
types	jewellery

Typical packaging containers in thermoformed polystyrene made by Sweetheart Plastics of Fareham, using BP Chemicals CP49 polystyrene.

ABS (Acrylonitrile butadiene styrene) Sometimes known as an 'engineer's plastics' because of its properties of toughness and impact resistance, ABS is a co-polymer of styrene, butadiene and acrilonitrile. The two latter components contribute the very much enhanced impact resistance which is the weak point of polystyrene.

Special characteristics:

extreme toughness	excellent impact
good dimensional	resistance
stability	not transparent
weather resistance	resistance to chemicals

Applications:

boat hulls	motor components
general vacuum forming	cases for consumer
	goods

SAN (styrene acrylonitrile) is another material, very close to ABS, possessing greater transparency and used for tableware, light fittings etc.

CELLULOSICS

The earliest thermoplastics were cellulose based and, although many of their original applications have been superseded, spectacle frames, tool handles etc. continue to be made in this material. Cellulosics generally have outstanding toughness and impact resistance. The two most usual materials encountered are cellulose acetate and

CAB (cellulose acetate butyrate). Both are produced with a high degree of gloss and transparency in a wide range of colours. Cellulose acetate in fibre form is Rayon.

CAUTION Cellulose nitrate is a variant whose weakness is high inflammability and, for this reason, it should never be used in any situation where it could provide a hazard. It can be recognized by the smell of camphor plasticizer. It is less common nowadays but, where doubt exists, it is best to test a small sample.

Special properties:
Cellulose acetate (CA)   high transparency
extreme toughness   similar to cellulose
made as film   nitrate but
                           self-extinguishing

CAB (cellulose acetate butyrate)
high transparency   excellent colour range
produced as film   toughness
good weather resistance
Cellulose nitrate (CN)
high flammability   can have variegated
extreme toughness   colours
lustrous   good transparency
                     discolours on ageing

Applications:
Cellulose acetate
cinematograph film   lamp/light fittings
spectacle frames   tool handles
theatrical films
CAB (cellulose acetate butyrate)
outdoor signs   lamp/light fittings
Cellulose nitrate (CN)
table tennis balls   handles for cutlery
piano keys

POLYAMIDES

Nylon There are several types of nylon, each one designated a number – 6, 66, 6.10 etc. – which relates to its chemical make-up, the number describing the carbon atoms in the reactants used to prepare the material.

Apart from its uses in filament form for textiles, nylon is used in engineering applications. The material tends to absorb moisture, although some stabilized grades may be obtained.

Two typical forms of nylon are illustrated: Above shows nylon in continuous filament form as supplied by ICI Plastics Division; Opposite shows a typical engineering application-mouldings in ICI's Maranyl nylon.

Special characteristics:
very hard and tough   moulds accurately and
low coeffcient of friction into thin sections
performance less   good wearing
  affected by   properties
  temperature than most
  plastics
Applications:
textiles   fishing line and
ropes   monofilaments
engineering components, cable covering
  bearings   electrical mouldings

PHENOLICS
Phenolic resins (phenol formaldehyde or PF resins) are the oldest type, commonly known as Bakelite. They are mainly of use to the industrial moulder and are invariably dark coloured.

AMINOS

This group contains the UF (urea formaldehyde) resins and the MF (melamine formaldehyde) resins. In the raw state, UF resins are very white and can therefore be coloured in a wide range of bright tints. This characteristic immediately distinguishes them from the PF type.

Special characteristics:

very hard and tough	moulds accurately and
excellent electrical	in thin sections
resistance	good abrasion resistance
good colour range	self-extinguishing

Applications:

UF resins	*MF resins*
electrical goods	handles for cooking
laminates	utensils
toilet goods	ash-trays
container closures	moulded tableware
adhesives	decorative laminates

EPOXIDES

Epoxy resins are yellowish liquids and, like polyester resins, they are 'cold setting'. They can be plated and will withstand relatively high working temperatures.

Special characteristics:

good adhesion to metals,	good chemical resistance
glass etc.	very tough
outstanding electrical	can be machined
resistance	
low shrinkage	

Applications:

electrical goods	potting or encapsulation
laminates for electrical	surface coatings,
casings	floorings
adhesives	mould making

ALKYDS

By far the largest application of polyesters lies in GRP (glass reinforced plastics) structures. The resins are liquids.

Special characteristics:

good chemical resistance	local strength can be
good dimensional	varied
stability	'cold setting', no
excellent strength weight	applied heat
ratio	necessary
	can be self-coloured

Applications:

glass fibre reinforced	flooring
structures	potting and
button casting	encapsulation

Special characteristics:

cheapness	good impact strength
high rigidity	for a thermoset
excellent chemical	excellent electrical
resistance	resistance
	easily moulded

Applications:

electrical insulators/	low stressed domestic/
components/switches	commercial goods
knobs and handles	

flexible foams	rigid foams
upholstery cushions	insulation in cold
acoustic filling	storage units
crash padding in motor	insulation in building
vehicles	buoyancy in water craft
general foam filling	

These three chairs made by Tangent Foams Ltd. have shells made of rigid polyurethane foam. All three are made in the same mould which is masked to give variants. *Photo: ICI Plastics Division*

POLYURETHANES

Urethane plastics are made by combining two components — isocyanates and polyols. Different characteristics can be produced by varying the quantities. Mainly they are used for producing foamed materials in both rigid and flexible grades.

Special characteristics:

high strength to weight ratio

good chemical resistance

not dissolved by polyesters

PART 2
GENERAL METHODS
OF FABRICATION

Chapter 4
Plastics in the Workshop

Plastics can be worked with usual wood or metal tools which have been properly prepared or adapted. Machining qualities vary, but generally thermoplastics can be worked with techniques which match those for aluminium.

The beginner is advised to practise on scrap material and even deliberately to flout the advice given in this chapter so that he can experience for himself the peculiarities and limits of plastics as they break down under the tool.

Plastics suitable for machining come in a variety of forms as listed in Table 2.

STRESSES AND STRAINS
Allowance for internal stresses in machining tolerances will not be necessary except for sophisticated work. Internal stresses are set up during the manufacturing process and these become 'locked in' on cooling. If a piece of acrylic is heated to softening point and allowed to cool slowly, it will inevitably change its dimensions. This is because the resoftened material has been moved by the previously 'locked in' stress. Stress relieving is possible for close tolerance work and advice should be sought from the material supplier.

Secondary stresses may be further induced locally by the effect of machining. These may not appear for some considerable time. In some materials, these appear as craze marks; in others, they may appear as discolorations or 'blooms'. Crazing can be brought on by solvents or even the vapours of solvents.

GENERAL RULES FOR MACHINING
Overheating In any machining operation heat is generated and this must be kept below the softening point of the plastic. If the plastic softens, it adheres to the tool or the surface or both. In either case, it causes binding which in turn creates greater friction.

The softening point of thermoplastics (which in some cases may only be around the boiling point of water) is very quickly achieved at the tip of a cutting tool and, because of

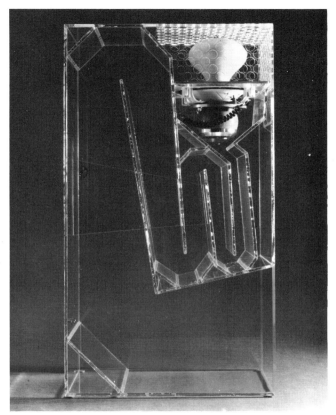

This loudspeaker enclosure in $\frac{1}{4}$" acrylic sheet embodies a compound folded horn which, it is claimed, is six times more efficient than conventional enclosures. Designed by K. Freivokh at the Royal College of Art.

Above Forms in Perspex acrylic which have been hand shaped and polished. Designed and made by Michael Dillon.

Different colours of Perspex acrylic sheet have been laminated by solvent cement, shaped by hand and polished. Designed by Michael Dillon.

low thermal conductivity, cannot easily be dissipated. Swarf makes a good guide; this should be crisp and clean cut. If it is soft and blurred, too much heat is being generated.

To keep the work cool, faces of tools which are in following contact with the plastic should never be rough, e.g., the lands of drills and the side faces of saws. Where possible, these should be ground narrower than the cutting edge.

When machining metals, lubricants are employed to protect the *tool*, but when machining plastics, they are used to protect the *material*. For this reason they are

imperative. Some soluble oils promote crazing, but thick soapy water is suitable for all plastics.

Clamping It is essential to hold work rigid, and sheet materials must be held so that they cannot flex or splintering will result. When sawing or drilling, the work must be supported underneath close to the cutting area. Double-sided adhesive tape can usefully be employed for holding sheet stock.

Tool preparation Generally, cutting edges should have little or no rake, or even a slightly negative forward rake. Back clearances should be allowed for. Surprisingly

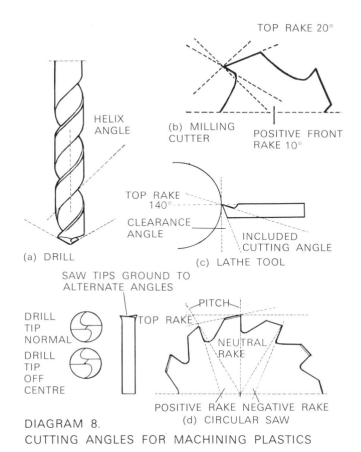

HELIX ANGLE

(a) DRILL

TOP RAKE 20°

(b) MILLING CUTTER

POSITIVE FRONT RAKE 10°

TOP RAKE 140°

CLEARANCE ANGLE

INCLUDED CUTTING ANGLE

(c) LATHE TOOL

SAW TIPS GROUND TO ALTERNATE ANGLES

DRILL TIP NORMAL

DRILL TIP OFF CENTRE

TOP RAKE

PITCH

NEUTRAL RAKE

POSITIVE RAKE   NEGATIVE RAKE

(d) CIRCULAR SAW

DIAGRAM 8.
CUTTING ANGLES FOR MACHINING PLASTICS

Sand box by Chic Taylor. Acrylic. *Photo: Alecto International.*

plastics soon blunt tools, particularly those with certain fillers added. For these, high-speed tools are recommended. Because of the build-up of static charges, clinging swarf may be a nuisance and a good anti-static material will obviate this.

DRILLING (See Diagram 8)

For soft plastics, drills with a slow spiral or helix angle and smooth wide flutes serve best. For all work, the point angle should be obtuse — up to 140°. This increases the 'slicing action' and is particularly necessary when drilling thin sheets; otherwise, there is a risk that the cutting point will pierce the sheet before the whole cutting edge of the drill has made contact, which can result in tearing. Holes drilled in most plastics come out slightly undersize because the material 'gives' under the cutting pressure. This accounts for the tight fit of a drill in its hole and allows the shank of the drill to be in rubbing contact with the sides of the hole. To avoid friction, lands can be ground back beyond the first $\frac{1}{2}$". Alternatively, the point may be ground to a slightly off centre chisel edge (see Diagram 8). This causes the drill to cut slightly oversize.

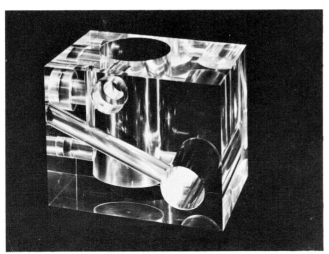

Valve body in acrylic material (Perspex) by Stanley Plastics Ltd.

Electric clock in Perspex acrylic sheet. Designed and made by Elizabeth Taylor, first-year student. *Photo: West Surrey College of Art and Design.*

SAWING

All saws are prone to overheat the plastics. The rate of feed and speed of cut can be critical and are best judged from experience. At all times the work must be supported against 'chatter'. Tallow is a suitable lubricant for all blades. Hand saws and jig saws can be used, blades with about twelve teeth per inch being most suitable. Very fine toothed blades tend to clog.

Circular saws The teeth must run true. The tip of each tooth should touch an imaginary circle; any one tooth projecting is likely to cause splintering. This irregularity can be trued by grinding on the machine itself.

For general work, negative rake and slight forward set are recommended.

Saws with a pitch of eight teeth per inch suit most materials, but those with five teeth per inch are more suitable for thick sections. Swarf is cleared more easily if the bases of the teeth are rounded. A hollow ground blade which is not in contact behind the cutting edge is preferred. Adhesive tape attached to both sides of the cutting line tends to obviate chipping.

Band saws For average thicknesses, twelve teeth per inch are recommended. For thicker grades, those with four or five teeth per inch may be better. Widely spaced teeth obviate clogging. In all cases, saw guides should be adjusted to a close fit to minimise 'waving'. Tallow is again a good dressing.

TURNING (See Diagram 8c)

A good cutting edge to the lathe tool is essential. For average work, 5° to 10° of top rake are recommended. At least 5° front rake is necessary to avoid overheating. The angle should not be too great, however, or the tool will soon blunt. Inadequate top rake causes splintering.

MILLING AND ROUTING

Cutters with up to 10° positive front rake and 20° top rake are recommended. For routing, normal, high speed, wood working tools are most suitable. Any type of cutter can be used, single or double edged, but it should be ground with a slight angle for back clearance.

SCREWING AND TAPPING

Standard taps and dies with coarse threads are generally most suitable. Because of the 'give' in plastics materials, tapped threads have a tight fit. Like drilled holes, they tend to turn out undersize. Self-tapping screws can only be used on non-brittle plastics where the thread can 'bite'. Where components are to be subjected to stress, it is preferable not to thread the plastic itself but to use a threaded metal insert.

FINISHING

Deep scratches must first be cut back with a sanding disc or scraper and the rough surface left, in turn, must be rubbed down with graded abrasive pastes. Dull surfaces can be brought to a high gloss with a calico buffing wheel and a gentle abrasive such as rouge or kieselguhr. Blemishes in highly polished materials such as acrylics are very noticeable and are even magnified by refraction.

ADHESIVES

Plastics may be joined together by adhesives and they may also be joined to other materials. The bond with some materials may be strong, with others it may be weak, and some materials cannot be bonded together at all. The effectiveness of an adhesive is dependent on such factors as temperature, porosity of the surfaces, fit and the load to which the joint is subjected.

To select a suitable adhesive for bonding two materials, see Table 4 for a bonding agent compatible with both adherents. For example, for rubber to polystyrene, the only suitable adhesive would be an epoxy. Then see Table 5 for a suitable brand.

Joint design For best performance, joints should be so designed that loads are evenly distributed over the whole of the interface. This condition is only entirely satisfied if the stress is in plain tension or shear. Stresses which tend to cleave or peel are likely to cause failure.

Cementing Thermoplastics may be joined by solvent cementing, a solvent of the polymer being employed. The disadvantage of pure solvents is that as they evaporate totally, no residue is left to take up any gaps in the join. The ideal solvent is one which dissolves rapidly and evaporates quickly so that the surfaces are attacked for the shortest time possible. However, the action must not be so quick that the join cannot properly be made before the surfaces have dried. Solvents for thermoplastics are listed in Table 6. It must be remembered that even the vapours of solvents can cause crazing. A good cement for acrylic can be made by dissolving chips of the polymer in glacial acetic acid, acetone or chloroform. Proprietary cements can also be obtained.

CAUTION Solvents are highly inflammable and may give off vapours which can cause sickness. Ventilation is essential. Glacial acetic acid may cause acid burns to the skin and should not be used in school or domestic situations.

Construction employing sheet plastics materials. Lux 12 by Schoffer. *Photo: Galerie Denise René, Paris.*

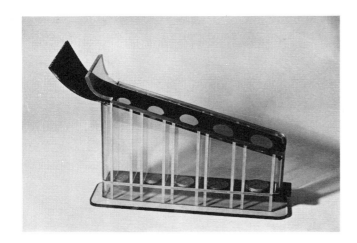

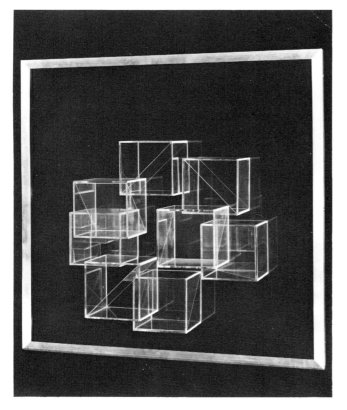

Left top: Money box in Perspex acrylic sheet by a Foundation student. *Photo: West Surrey College of Art and Design.*

Left: Space cube structure. Clear Perspex in a black box with metal frame. Peter Clapham. *Photo: Marlborough Fine Art Ltd.*

Above: Acrylic component with pierced flanges, threads etc. made by Stanley Plastics Ltd.

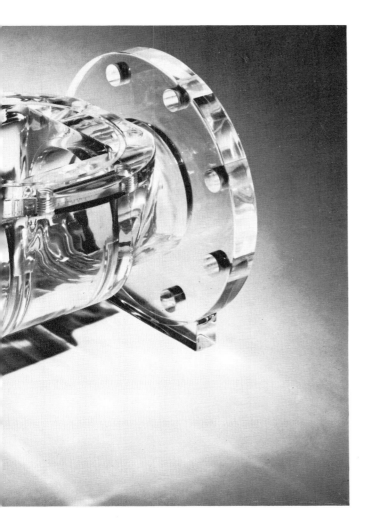

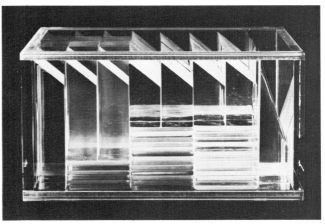

Right top: Minimum chess set by David Pelham. Perspex. The photograph illustrates how the various pieces fit together. *Photo by courtesy of Alecto International.*

Right bottom: Chair with formed acrylic back. Designed and made by pupils of the Sir Frederic Osborn School, Welwyn Garden City. *Photo: Mr. A. Harness.*

Top left: Illuminated mural in acrylic. C. A. Meredith.

Middle left: Oddments of polystyrene sheet donated by a local manufacturer are solvent cemented into a sculpture.

Left: Pressed dishes made by pupils of the Sir Frederic Osborn School, Welwyn Garden City. *Photo: Mr. A. Harness.*

Above: Plastics construction, *Carrés-en-vibration*, by Soto. *Photo: Galerie Denise René, Paris.*

DIAGRAM 9. MASKING FOR
SOLVENT CEMENTS

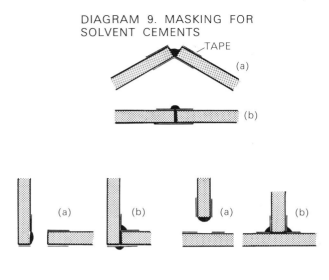

DIAGRAM 10.

LAMINATING

Laminating Where flat surfaces have to be joined, it is possible to pour cement on to one surface and to bring the other down on to it, as in Diagram 10b. When pressure is applied, the cement is squeezed out of the sides leaving a bubble free joint. For larger surfaces, it is advisable to lay the pool of cement along one edge and to bring the surfaces into contact, driving the pool forward (see Diagram 10a). It is essential to clamp up joints until they have dried, but excessive force squeezes out too much material and can cause stress. Various effects can be achieved by colouring the cements, artists' colours generally being suitable. Pure solvents may also be used for laminating; the faces of the plastics may be softened by laying them on strips of felt soaked in solvent.

Coloured or patterned sheet is generally available in thin sections, but by laminating together coloured and patterned sheets, optical effects can be achieved — especially when lit from the edge. Laminations which have been properly made should be invisible except when viewed edgewise, when slight optical distortion may be unavoidable.

As the slightest trace of solvent produces an unsightly blemish, it is vital to mask areas around a join which might become spoiled. Naturally, the masking must be done with a material which is not itself affected and scotch tape is generally suitable. Diagram 9 shows typical methods of masking joints with tape. When the tape is removed, the excess cement is removed with it.

Solvent cements are quick acting, and it is not always easy to cover a large surface before they have evaporated. If a skin has started to form on either surface, the resultant join will be the weaker for it.

Some ingenuity may be required to coat complex edge shapes, but it is sometimes possible to dip them in a layer of solvent poured on to glass. For accurate control, a hypodermic syringe can be used.

Chapter 5
Thermoforming

USING A HAND TORCH

When sculptors work in plastics, they often use techniques which would be considered highly irregular in industrial circles. What in the world of commerce is a fault or blemish, for the artist may be an effect to be exploited. Attractive textures can be produced by controlled overheating or deliberate solvent attack.

Examples of the work of Ferris Newton, who has worked extensively in thermoplastics, are included to show the range of forms and effects which can be achieved using nothing more than a gas torch and rudimentary hand tools.

The usual butane torch with rechargeable cylinders is most convenient, but the type of torch selected is not critical. When softened, the plastic sheet can be manipulated by hand and joins can be made by softening two edges and pressing them together. When working with

plastics in this way, their low thermal conductivity, perhaps uniquely, is an advantage; local areas can be heated without risk of collapsing the whole structure.

CAUTION Those wishing to work with an open flame should note that:
  (a) Noxious fumes may be given off, so good ventilation is essential.
  (b) Plastics vary in the way they burn (see Table 7), and there should be adequate facilities to smother any accidental fire.

Manufacturers, in their technical data, do not recommend a material as being suitable for welding unless the breaking strength of the weld is above certain limits and can be described as permanent. For much artistic work, or for applications where stress is not a problem, these criteria may not apply, and materials which are not normally recommended can be used. Sample testing will determine those which are suitable.

Where their melting points are more or less compatible, it is not impossible sometimes to induce plastics of different types to join, but mostly this is not practical. Various grades and colours of a similar material can be joined more readily.

OVENS

General requirements Sheet materials for manual forming are softened in an oven. Any type of oven can be used, including a domestic oven, providing it reaches the required temperature, though best results are obtained from those which are purpose built. The oven should be capable of close temperature control between 120°C and 170°C, should have an even distribution of heat with no hot or cold spots, and should have no chinks for cold draughts. Preferably, there should be provision on the inside to support flat sheets as well as three-dimensional objects.

Notes for home constructors The size of oven which can be heated from given elements and loadings will depend on such factors as insulation qualities, freedom from draughts, frequency with which the door is opened etc., so it is not possible to make a recommendation for all circumstances. For average workshop purposes, 3kw is sufficient for an oven measuring 3' × 2' × 1' and 6kw (normal British domestic cooker supply) is suitable for one measuring 3' × 2' × 2'.

Diagram 11a shows a typical arrangement for a 6kw oven of the recirculatory type, and Diagram 11b shows a 3kw fan-assisted oven.

Simple exercise in thermoforming, designed and made by a sixteen-year-old.

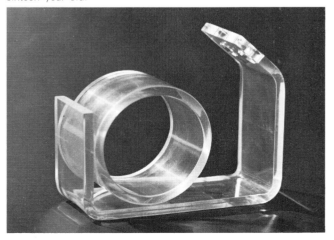

Home constructors should seek the advice of a qualified electrical engineer to supervise work on the electrics.

Frames are best made of welded angle iron, although bolted slotted angle may be employed. The panels may be of sheet metal or an asbestos-based insulation material such as Marinite. The door should be sealed with asbestos string and arranged with a stay and toggle type fasteners so that it can be opened and closed quickly with one hand and with minimum heat loss. It is strongly recommended that a cut-out switch is fitted to the door so that the supply is isolated when the oven is open. The inner shelves may be in metal or asbestos and should be well pierced to assist circulation. If the interior is lined with reflective aluminium foil such as is used in kitchens, the efficiency of the oven will be considerably increased.

Temperature control An oven may be controlled manually by switching on and off against a thermometer, but it is not advisable to use a mains switch for this purpose. The Sun Vic type of energy regulator, type Ery/Erc, can be in-

Thermoforming oven made at West Surrey College of Art and Design.

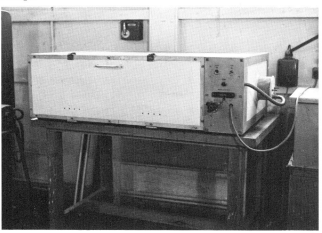

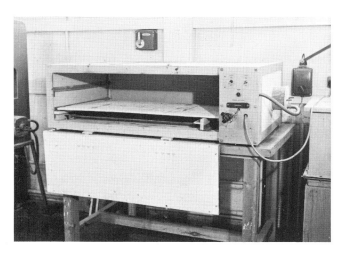

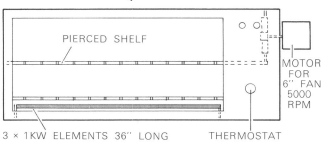

MOTOR FOR FAN

PIERCED SHELVES

HEATING ELEMENTS

DIAGRAM 11a.
TYPICAL LAYOUT FOR HEAT EXCHANGER OVEN 6KW

PIERCED SHELF

MOTOR FOR 6" FAN 5000 RPM

3 × 1KW ELEMENTS 36" LONG   THERMOSTAT

DIAGRAM 11b. TYPICAL LAYOUT FOR FAN ASSISTED OVEN 3KW 6 CUBIC FEET

corporated in the circuit. When set against a thermometer, these are very satisfactory. For a 6kw oven, two such regulators will be needed.

Temperature distribution The most satisfactory means of ensuring an even temperature all over the inside of the oven is to keep the air constantly on the move. By this means, hot and cold spots are scavenged and temperature differences of less than plus or minus 2°C are possible. For most practical purposes it is enough to include an efficient fan in a suitable position on the inside. This creates sufficient turbulence to ensure good temperature distribution. It is possible, however, to build an oven of the heat exchanger type where the heat source is remote from the chamber and where the air is constantly cycled over the heat source, round the oven and back again. In this case, electric elements are usually placed in the air stream. Diagram 11a shows the circulation of air in an oven of this type.

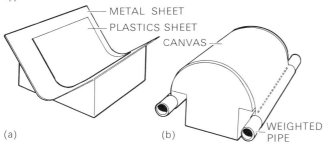

(a)   (b)

DIAGRAM 12.   TYPICAL FORMERS FOR SHAPING THERMOPLASTICS SHEET

OVEN FORMING

Single curvature forms   (Diagram 12) Single curvature forms present little problem. The heated plastic sheet can be suspended by two edges and allowed to sag inside a form or it can be draped over it (see Diagram 12a, b). A curved photographic glazing sheet provides a good surface which can be bent to any desired form. Alternatively, marking of the plastics will be minimized if the sheet is covered with a piled cloth. For accurate impressions, the plastics must be held in contact with the former and this can be achieved with a weighted cloth as in Diagram 12b.

CLAMP AND TEMPLATE TECHNIQUES

Complex forms can be made out of flat sheet by using templates set in frames as in Diagram 13. The frame may be of wood, in which case a quick release clamping system is essential, so that when the softened plastics is withdrawn

DIAGRAM 13. CLAMP AND TEMPLATE TECHNIQUES

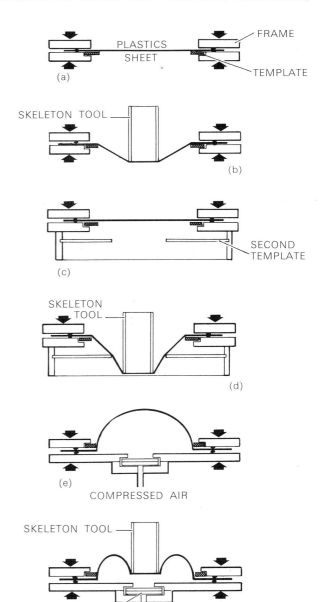

from the oven, it can be clamped up very quickly ready for forming. But it is much better if the frame is metal, so that it can be heated with the plastics.

Diagrams 13a to f illustrate a variety of forms which can be made using this simple equipment. Diagram 13a shows a heated plastics sheet clamped into a frame over a template so that the edges are firmly held. Diagram 13b shows how a skeleton tool, which in this case could be the rim of a can, is used to press the plastics into form. Sheet material for the template can be hardboard, wood or metal, but it is important that the edge of the hole cut in it is well finished, otherwise the plastics may be marked. A secure system of clamps is essential, and while various spring-loaded types may be used, the De-sta-co toggle clamps of the portable pliers type are most effective.

Diagrams 13c and 13d show how more than one template can be used to achieve more complex forms. Alternative frame sections showing various systems for gripping the plastics are shown in Diagram 14.

Whenever male tools are used for returned forms, they are best made up out of $\frac{3}{32}$'' metal strip as skeleton outlines only. Printers' rule, as used for die-cutting, is suitable. This material is easily bent to shape and such tools have the advantage that only a small area of the rim touches the surface, so the risk of chilling or spoiling the plastics is lessened. They may even be used in conjunction with a female form as in Diagram 15.

Blow forming Diagrams 13e and 13f show how a clamp can be adapted as a blowing frame by replacing one side with a base-board to which is attached an air line. The heated plastics is swiftly clamped up and compressed air fed in via a valve until the required form has been achieved. Again, more complex returned forms are possible as shown in Diagram 13f.

Note that it is advisable to provide a chamber containing

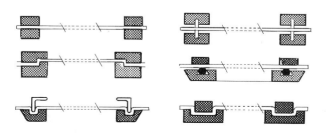

DIAGRAM 14. VARIOUS CLAMPING SYSTEMS

DIAGRAM 15. SKELETON TOOL FORMING

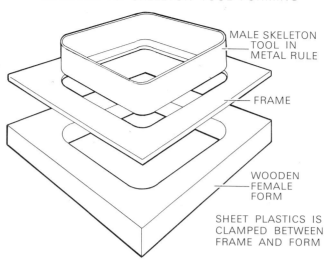

MALE SKELETON TOOL IN METAL RULE

FRAME

WOODEN FEMALE FORM

SHEET PLASTICS IS CLAMPED BETWEEN FRAME AND FORM

wadding in the base-board. If this is not included, the blast of cold air rapidly cools the area of plastics where it impinges, which results in deformed shapes. An alternative blowing table is shown in Diagram 16, with a universal clamp system so that frames of varying thicknesses can be inserted.

CAUTION Any devices which are attached to compressed air systems must be capable of withstanding the considerable pressures involved: if a container bursts, the effect could be serious. Expert advice should be sought to verify that home constructed machines are safe.

A COMBINED BLOWING AND FORMING MACHINE
(Diagram 16)

For a general description of the vacuum forming process, reference should be made to Chapter 13.

The machine depicted in Diagram 16 can easily be constructed in the workshop. The heater is designed to swivel so that it serves not only to heat the vacuum frame but also to heat material on the blowing table. If it is unplugged, it serves as a portable multi-purpose heater.

The machine can be built to various sizes depending on the heater elements chosen, but the smallest advised is 2kw. A grill heater from a domestic cooker can be in-

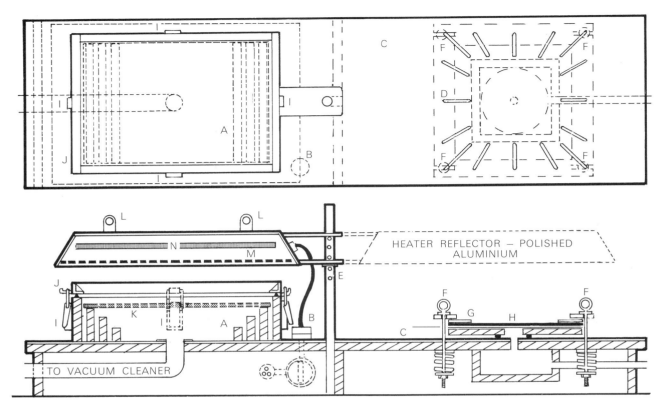

DIAGRAM 16. COMBINED VACUUM/BLOWING MACHINE

corporated at this rating to provide a maximum heated area of about 15" × 10". If $2\frac{1}{2}$kw elements are used, the area can be increased to about 18" × 12". Holes are provided in the vertical heater support to vary the height and thus the temperature at the surface of the plastics. The vacuum clamping frame is secured by four toggle latches (typically Dzuz TL or Camloc 51L types), two of which may be of the

hinged variety. They should all be adjustable to accommodate various thicknesses of plastics. As there is no rising table, provision must be made to accommodate moulds of different thicknesses. The simplest way is to include loose wooden supports on which the table can be varied in height. The blowing table is provided with a series of slots to engage clamps, thus allowing frames of varying sizes to be

Blow-forming table made at West Surrey College of Art and
Design, using De-sta-co clamps.

accommodated. If the blowing frame is made of metal,
which is strongly recommended, the plastics can be
heated after it has been clamped up.

Improvised compressed air A source of compressed air is
desirable, and if necessary a system can be improvised from
an old motor tyre and foot-pump as in Diagram 17.

HEATED TOOLS

A piece of sufficiently hot metal applied to plastics will
soften it, and the principle is applied in a variety of welding
and shaping tools. Simple tools can be heated in an open
flame, but proprietary tools are fitted with an electric
cartridge heater.

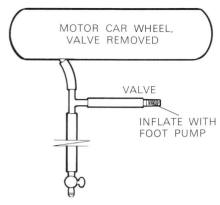

MOTOR CAR WHEEL,
VALVE REMOVED

VALVE

INFLATE WITH
FOOT PUMP

DIAGRAM 17. IMPROVISED COMPRESSED AIR

Heating mirrors These are slabs of metal, usually aluminium, with the surfaces machined to a good finish with provision for heating to softening temperatures of plastics. One edge is usually chamfered for heating narrow strips. A simple weld is made by holding two edges of plastics against the hot surface and pressing them together when soft. Typical joints are shown in Diagram 18.

To prevent adhesions, it is normal to sheath the metal in PTFE (polytetrafluoroethylene). Mirrors are usually electrically heated, though the versatile Leister Kombi tool is heated by hot air. (This is a multi-purpose tool with

Below left: Decorating a thermoplastic sheet with relief. Local areas have been softened with the open flame of the hand torch and impressed with wooden dowels.

Below: Softening thermoplastics sheet on a heating mirror.

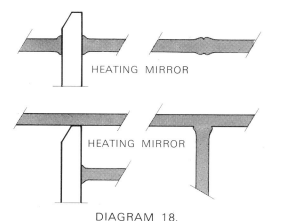

DIAGRAM 18.
BUTT JOINT AND T JOINT USING HEATING MIRROR

attachments suitable for a wide range of work in thermo-plastics.)

Various types of mirror are produced commercially which are adapted to specific applications, e.g. for joining lengths of PVC pipe, and when buying a mirror it is essential to select one which is appropriate to the need. For general craft work or for sculptural purposes, a plate size up to 10" square will be adequate. Alternatively, an old domestic iron or a photographic dry mounter can be adapted, and if even these are not available, a thick metal plate mounted over a heater will serve.

BENDING SHEET PLASTICS

To bend sheet plastics, it is necessary to confine the heating to the area of the bend. With care, bends up to 18" long may be made with a hand torch, the area not to be heated being protected by Marinite boards. The main difficulty with the hand torch is sustaining an adequate

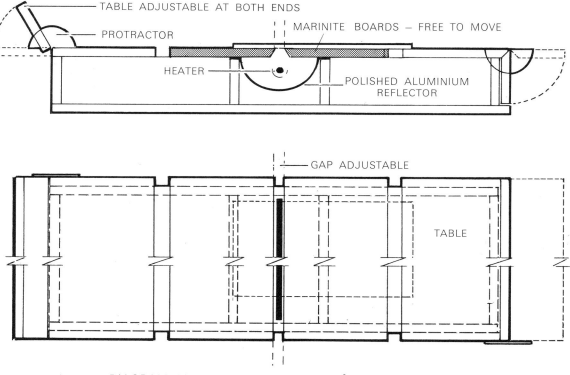

DIAGRAM 19. COMBINED STRIP HEATER AND BENDER

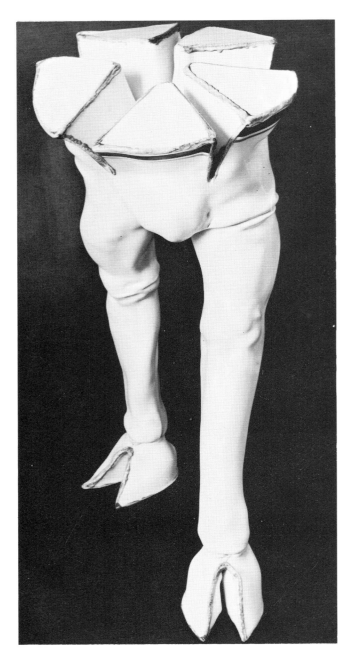

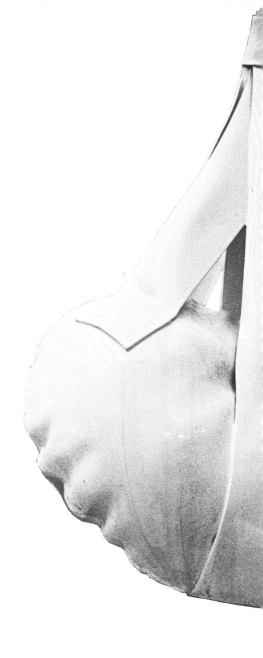

Free sculptures made of thermoplastics sheet, formed by hand in the open flame of a torch. Ferris Newton.

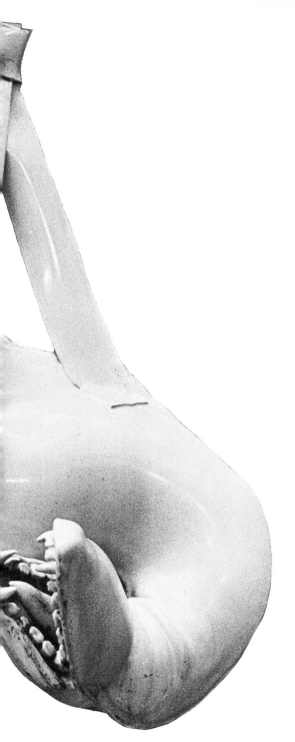

temperature along the whole of the length. Thick materials may require heating from both sides. For longer lengths and for better control, a purpose designed strip heater can be made up.

CAUTION Asbestos/cement materials should not be used in any application which involves direct heating. They may disintegrate with some force. Proprietary materials such as Marinite should be used.

CONSTRUCTING A STRIP HEATER
Diagram 19 shows a typical construction. No specific size is detailed; heaters rated at about 1kw per yard are recommended, and the constructor can thus calculate his own measurements.

The width of the heated area can be adjusted by varying the gap between the Marinite boards. Provision is made for the table to be tilted at either end for inside or outside angles, and if protractors are attached, the angle of bend can be accurately controlled.

Chapter 6
Welding Plastics

Inflatable boat designed and made by John Martin, first-year student: *Photo: West Surrey College of Art and Design.*

THE HOT AIR PROCESS

Thermoplastics soften at comparatively low temperatures and easily burn in an open flame. Clearly what is needed for welding is a gentle flow of heat at a somewhat lower temperature, and this can be obtained by the hot air process. It is not dissimilar to metal welding, except that hot air is used instead of a flame and a plastic filler rod is used instead of a metal one.

A controlled flow of air is passed over an electric heater and thence directed by a hand-held nozzle to the surfaces to be joined. Usually the nozzle is incorporated in a welding torch which also contains a cartridge-type heater element. Compressed air at up to 15 lb. per sq in. and at $\frac{1}{2}$ cu. ft. per minute is desirable for general purpose work. It is usual to fit a rate of flow meter. A typical arrangement is shown in Diagram 20. Where a compressed air supply is not available, torches may be purchased which contain a built-in blower unit (Leister Kombi).

Hot air tools are produced for industrial purposes in a wide range of types with special attachments for particular operations. For normal bench working where speed is not important, a simple torch as shown in Diagram 20 is all that is needed.

Types of weld Before commencing welding, the surfaces must be quite dry and free of grease. The edges to be joined should then be chamfered to about 65°. The 'valley' thus created when they are offered up will be filled with the filler rod (Diagram 21a). It is best to leave a slight gap so that the filler can penetrate thoroughly. A stronger joint is obtained in thick material by welding both sides (Diagrams 21c, f). It is essential that the sheets to be welded should be held quite firm. A long weld may require the edges to be tack welded together to locate them and prevent warping during the operation.

Technique The end of the filler rod is softened in the hot air and pressed into the 'start' of the welding 'trough'. With the rod held *vertically*, hot air is directed in a rotary action over the filler rod and the sheet together. The distance away will be determined by the temperature of the air and the type of

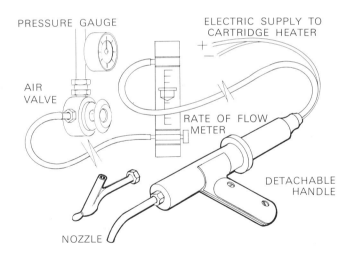

DIAGRAM 20. HOT AIR WELDING KIT

plastics, but on average, one to two inches will be suitable.

A steady pressure, also near vertical, is maintained on the filler rod until it softens and collapses into the trough. If the sheet material has also been correctly softened, the two will bond together. The skill lies in heating the rod and the

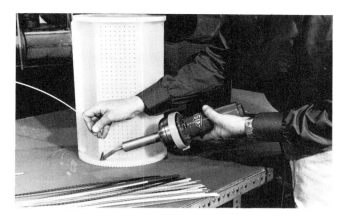

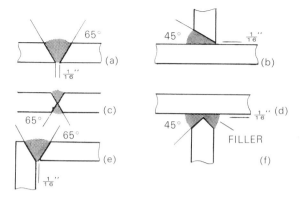

DIAGRAM 21. TYPICAL HOT AIR WELDS

Left: The Leister Combi tool works on the hot air principle, and as it contains its own impeller, it does not require a compressed air system. It can be used for welding or for thermoforming.

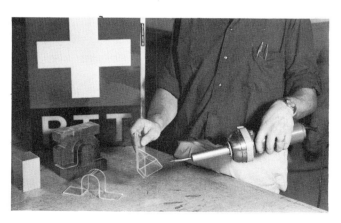

bed of the weld sufficiently and evenly but without overdoing it. The speed of the weld can be felt and governed by the rate at which the softened rod collapses and fuses in the 'bed'. The rod should not be forced to collapse; a gentle steady pressure only is required.

Slight darkening or 'browning' of the edges of the heated area is acceptable, but it indicates that the upper temperature limits have been achieved and that burning of the plastics will result if the heating is prolonged.

Thick materials form a large 'trough' and it may take several runs of weld to fill it up.

Manufacturers list special filler rods against particular plastics, but these are generally not essential; a narrow strip sawn from the edge of the sheet itself will, for most purposes, serve just as well.

If the bench surface is a good conductor of heat, it will tend to absorb heat from the plastics making the process more difficult.

FRICTION WELDING

Welds in circular-sectioned rigid materials can often be carried out by this process. The two surfaces to be joined are rotated against each other under pressure and at high speed. The resultant frictional heat softens the materials so that they fuse. When the softened surfaces are allowed to cool, a very strong bond is obtained. An oscillating motion can be used for welding non-circular components. Ordinary lathes or pillar drills can be adapted to the purpose, providing there is a friction clutch or some provision to allow both components to rotate together freely once the joint has fused.

One chief advantage of the system is that because of the low thermal conductivity and the high local intensity of the frictional heat, the fusion temperatures at the rubbing surfaces are quickly reached, but the temperature of the bulk of the material remains unchanged.

The surfaces need not be prepared, and as some of the material is squeezed out of the sides of the weld, there are no gap filling problems.

It is not possible to recommend speeds and pressures; they are best discovered by working up from moderate to high. They can always be increased until fusion is effected.

CAUTION Work must be securely clamped and aligned and protective goggles worn, particularly when working brittle materials, for there is a risk of shattering.

Joint design When joining circular sections, it is advisable to curve both faces slightly so that they are proud in the

Welding the edges of an inflatable PVC cushion. The decoration has been pre-printed by silk-screen process. A jaw-type impulse welder is being used.

The completed cushion being inflated.

(a)   (b)

DIAGRAM 22. FRICTION WELDING

centre (see Diagram 22a). This ensures that when they are brought together, the centre parts touch and fuse before the outer parts come into contact. This minimizes the effect of the speed differential. The rule in preshaping sections to be friction welded is: maximum area to the weld surface and minimum speed differential across the weld surface. To achieve this, 'stepped' or 'tongue and grooved' sections can be employed, as in Diagram 22b.

WELDING PLASTIC FILM, INFLATABLES
The flexibility of plastics film or sheet depends upon the amount of plasticizer included in the original mix. Those with most plasticizer are the softest and weld more easily because their softening temperatures are lower and allow the material to flow with less chance of degradation. The

welding of a pre-printed or decorated material may present problems if the ink is not of a type which can be absorbed into the bond. Inks containing heavy or metallic powders are particularly prone to give trouble.

There is no clear distinction between what are called in

the industry films, foils or sheets, but thin sheets would approximate to thicknesses above .020" (postcard thickness), films from .005" upwards, and anything thinner than .005" would be termed a foil. It is possible to make satisfactory welded joints in all these thicknesses in most thermoplastic materials.

The low thermal conductivity of plastics has already been discussed and it is a fundamental impediment to welding. When two overlapping surfaces have to be joined, it is necessary to soften both so that they can fuse together under pressure. It is important to note that it is the *interface*, rather than the outsides, which has to be softened for satisfactory fusion to take place. Heat applied to the outer surfaces achieves nothing so long as the interface remains cool. Because of the low thermal conductivity, heat applied to the outer surface takes so long to penetrate that there is a risk that the interface will still be cool even after the outer surface has become degraded.

Films and foils, because of their thinness, do not present too much of a problem in this respect. On the other hand, their very thinness means that the slightest overheating can lead to their total destruction. The ideal would be to use a means of heating the films evenly throughout, or with maximum temperature at the interface, and then to clamp the surfaces together until they are cool. Clamping during the cooling period is essential, because under the influence of heat, stresses in the plastic are released and the material distorts.

HEAT SEALING
Heated tools The simplest heat-sealing tool comprises a metal 'shoe' attached to a cartridge heater. Such a tool can be improvised by attaching thick wire to the end of a soldering iron.

In some cases, a joint may be difficult to make if the tool is applied to the outside of the material. Lapped joints, made by passing the tool between the surfaces following on the outside with a roller, should then be attempted. In all cases, it is essential that the shoe is highly polished. If it is too hot, the film can easily be destroyed. When a tool is applied to the outer surface, it is helpful to place a barrier film such as polyester (Melinex), which has a higher melting point, between the material and the tool. The barrier film is less likely to melt and so protects the joint even if it has been overheated.

A variety of tools for film sealing are shown in Diagram 23. These are generally suitable for sealing materials up to .060". Materials suitable for heat sealing are listed in Table 3.

DIAGRAM 23.
TYPICAL HEATED TOOLS

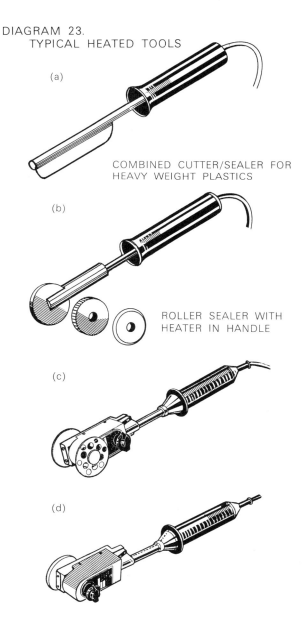

(a)

COMBINED CUTTER/SEALER FOR HEAVY WEIGHT PLASTICS

(b)

ROLLER SEALER WITH HEATER IN HANDLE

(c)

(d)

(c) and (d) 'THECO' ROLLER SEALERS THERMOSTATICALLY CONTROLLED

Portable impulse welder made in Germany. *Photo: Parnall and Sons.*

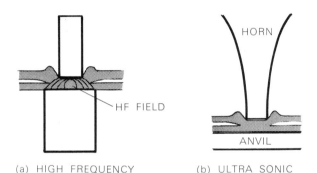

(a) HIGH FREQUENCY   (b) ULTRA SONIC

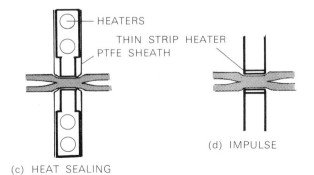

(c) HEAT SEALING   (d) IMPULSE

DIAGRAM 24. TYPES OF WELD FOR FLEXIBLE
PLASTICS

HEAT SEALERS

The principle of the heat sealer is that an electrical resistor heats a narrow metal bar which in turn heats the plastics (see Diagram 24c). The most common, among the portable types at least, is the 'jaw' type in which two heated platens are brought together in a pincer movement, pressure being sustained until the joint has been both heated and cooled.

For industrial applications, heat sealers are specially adapted for specific tasks: polythene bag manufacture, packaging, horticultural etc., and among those which are made for general work in packaging, there are many which are suitable for general craft work. Their main limitation for creative work is that they are produced with straight heaters only.

For most work, it is essential that the sealer incorporates an electric timer and temperature controller so that the optimum settings can be selected and repeated.

Industrial machines, designed for long production runs, may use the heated tool principle in other ways: some incorporate rotary sealers where the film is passed at high speed between two hot metal rollers, others utilize two endless belts which carry the plastic through heating and cooling zones while applying pressure.

IMPULSE SEALING

The impulse sealer may look like and be operated in a similar way to the heat sealer, but the important difference lies in the element. The impulse sealer has an element of low thermal inertia, usually a thin metal tape. This, because of its low mass, can be brought to temperature and cooled again in a matter of seconds (see Diagram 24d). It is essential that tools of this type incorporate a timer to adjust the period of heating; this is critical between different grades and thicknesses of plastic. As with heat sealing, it is necessary to maintain pressure over the joint until it has cooled.

It is not unusual with this type of heater to find that the jaws are not protected by PTFE. The cycle is so quick that the element is cool at the point of separation from the plastics.

Those most suitable for general bench work will be found among those produced for packaging. Without doubt, the impulse sealer is likely to be the most useful and versatile tool for general craft and workshop use.

HIGH FREQUENCY WELDING

The problems which arise in the working of plastics due to their low thermal conductivity have already been emphasized, and all the processes for heating plastics which have so far been described operate on the principle of the transference of heat by conduction, radiation or convection.

The high frequency process, however, works on a different principle and is generally used in industry whenever it is necessary to heat up a material which is itself a poor conductor of heat. Instead of applying heat to the outer surface, electrical energy is passed through the material and is converted to heat inside. When films are to be joined, they are placed under pressure between two electrodes capable of producing a high frequency field. The high frequency radiation passes throughout the joint, causing a violent molecular vibration similar to that which is obtained when the material is heated (see Diagram 24a). Thus the temperature of the joint is raised evenly throughout its thickness. Clamping is still necessary to hold the material until it is cold.

The generator needed to 'drive' this equipment is mains operated and usually bulky, so that few pieces of equipment can be considered portable, even though various hand-held, jaw-type electrodes can be operated from the generator. Very accurate control of temperature and of rate of temperature rise is possible, and when the current is switched off, heating immediately stops: no further temperature rise takes place due to absorption from neighbouring materials. The process is not very effective with polythene (polyethylene), but where it can be applied, extremely strong welds can be produced.

Materials with metallic inks or carbon black inks tend to induce arcing because of their high conductivity.

Some materials are treated for anti-static by incorporating chemicals into the mix, others may have an anti-static film applied to the surface. Both these types could prove troublesome to weld by the HF process.

Production machines are usually fitted with two platens mounted horizontally and capable of coming together under pressure. Skeleton forms in the shapes of the required welds are made up out of rule and mounted to the upper platen. The HF field is produced between the form and the lower platen. Forms made of rule are accurately made and can be set up to close tolerances so that both welding and cutting out operations can be simultaneous. Rule is produced in a variety of types to produce cut, serrated or plain welding edges.

Materials suitable for HF welding are given in Table 3.

ULTRASONIC WELDING
Ultrasonic or US welding is often confused with the HF welding process, but although it utilizes HF electrical

energy, US welding is a mechanical process.

The material to be welded is placed between a base plate known as an 'anvil' and a 'horn'. The horn, a specially shaped piece of metal, is connected to a transducer capable of causing it to oscillate at very high frequency. A weld is made by bringing the horn to bear and setting it to vibrate under pressure (see Diagram 24b). The mechanical vibrations it produces are transmitted through the material to the interface, where the friction of the two surfaces converts the vibrational energy into heat. Sufficient heat is generated to raise the temperature to the melting point of plastics in seconds, and one great advantage of the system is that the heat is restricted to the welding area.

Some types of equipment are relatively portable, but all types possess, besides the operating components, an electrical generator which produces electrical energy in the ultrasonic range and a transducer which converts this HF electrical energy into HF mechanical oscillations.

The ability of a material to be US welded depends upon how easily it transmits the vibrations to the interface; some materials tend to absorb the energy. The coefficient of friction also plays a part.

In some conditions, it is possible to 'weld' plastics to fibrous materials — even card. The softened plastics, under pressure, infiltrates the fibres and makes a 'bond'. It is also possible, sometimes, to weld different kinds of plastics — at least those with comparable melting points.

MELTED STRIP SEALING
This process is used industrially; portable tools for this process are not available. A fine bead of molten plastics is extruded on to the foils along the line to be sealed. Heat from the extruded material penetrates the foils so that both they and the bead are fused together. The chief advantage of the process is that the area of the weld, being thicker than the films rather than thinner, is immensely strong. It is also a very rapid process.

Chapter 7
Printing, Decoration and Surface Treatment of Plastics

It is only fairly recently that techniques for printing some types of plastics have been perfected: for a long time, problems of ink adhesion proved so troublesome that printing, with any degree of control at any rate, was out of the question. Because many plastics are highly resistant to chemical attack, it is not always easy to devise suitable solvent-based inks. Also, in many cases, the nature of the surface is such that it defies 'wetting'; any liquid applied to the surface 'crawls' into droplets. However these difficulties have now been overcome to such an extent that 'difficult' materials such as polythene (polyethylene) are printed in large quantities.

INK SELECTION
Each type of plastics demands its own special ink formulation. Inks which are solvent-based are easily formulated and are readily available for cellulosics, polystyrene and acrylics. Polystyrene is receptive to a wide range of solvent-based inks which are produced for normal screen printing processes. Some solvent-based inks can be used on some forms of ABS (acrylonitrile butadiene styrene). Solvent-based inks are easy to use, and because they etch the surface of the plastics and produce a chemical type of bond, generally do not present problems of adhesion.

On the other hand, solvent inks when printed on to thin sheet or film can cause puckering and distortion. This is because the material becomes softened and the molecular arrangement is disturbed. Excess solvent can lead to total breakdown of the material or crazing of the surface.

Polythene (polyethylene) cannot normally be printed without prior surface treatment: its surface is very smooth and offers no mechanical adhesion, and its chemical structure is such that chemical bonding is also difficult. Pre-treatment normally consists of oxidizing the surface layer of the film so that a different chemical structure, more appropriate for chemical bonding, is created. This is achieved industrially in a variety of ways: acid etching, flaming, chlorination, or by passing an electrical discharge over the surface.

The most convenient and inexpensive technique for the small workshop, and that which is generally used, is 'flaming'. The operation consists simply of passing the sheet through a flame. Simple equipment operating from mains gas can easily be set up. Burners which produce a good spread of flame of a hot oxidizing type with a blue centre should be selected. Some experimentation will be necessary to obtain optimum results, the variables being the time of exposure to the flame, the distance from the flame and the ratio of gas and air.

The effectiveness of the treatment can be determined by wetting sheets, which have been partly treated, with cold water. The water should easily wet the treated part of the surface and not break up into globules for about twenty seconds. On the other hand, the untreated area would be expected to reject immediately any wetting action and the water remain in droplets.

Polypropylene can also be flame-treated, although it is usually given a primer coat containing a solvent.

Some manufacturers produce proprietary inks which do not require pre-treatment: these may have limited resistance to wear on some materials.

Materials which contain a high proportion of plasticizer, such as a very flexible PVC, may give rise to problems of ink adhesion and peeling because the plasticizers have a tendency to migrate to the surface of the material.

APPLICATION OF INKS
Plastics are printed commercially by the usual processes: letterpress, gravure, lithography and silk-screen. Of these, the silk-screen process is the easiest and most versatile for small scale or limited run production.

Screen printing The surface of plastics is impervious; no ink is absorbed. This means that the printed image sits on *top* of the plastics and there is the danger that if the image takes too long to dry, it will 'flow out' and become blurred. To combat this, a quick drying ink is desirable, but this must not be so quick drying as to cause problems in screen clogging. Sometimes the image can be force dried by a hot air dryer.

The material to be printed must be mounted rigidly; films should be so attached that they do not 'creep' under the action of the squeegee, and sheet stock should be firmly attached to the baseboard. If this is not done, the material will rise with the screen and 'whiskers' of ink may form

Polystyrene sheet engraved with a stylus, inlaid, painted and post formed into relief. Designed by Haydon Williams.

around the image as it suddenly snaps apart. Problems of static may also arise and even be induced by the action of parting the screen from the surface.

The screen itself should be mounted so that it stands off the surface of the material by, say, $\frac{3}{16}''$. This ensures that only the area of the squeegee is in contact with the plastics. If the whole surface of the screen is in contact, there is a danger that the mesh itself will drag fractionally under the squeegee action and blur the area of image already printed.

ART WORK ON SHEET PLASTICS

Inks can be applied to plastics by any of the orthodox techniques: roller printing, painting, stippling, wiping, sponging etc. Alternatively, a surface ink coating can be applied by roller and a design scribed through the layer to expose the plastics underneath.

If resists are applied, the material can be dipped or otherwise coated.

Stencilled patterns can be produced by cutting shapes in any of the proprietary adhesive backed films and attaching to the plastics surface. If, after colouring, the film is peeled away, a crisp edged image is produced.

Polished sheet plastics provide an excellent surface for working with a point in the manner of an engraving; clean cut and very fine lines can be produced. If the sheet is then inked and the surface wiped clean, a crisp image, inlaid with ink, remains.

Decorated transparent sheets can be mounted in such a way that one image is viewed through another.

A variety of 'craft type' printing techniques from non-rigid surfaces, such as lino cutting and gelatine relief, are possible.

POST FORMING DECORATIVE RELIEFS

Perhaps the most significant property of a decorated thermoplastics sheet, the property which sets it apart from other sheet materials, is the ease with which it can be post formed into a relief. Indeed, this would appear to be the prime reason for choosing to decorate a plastics sheet in the first place.

There is no doubt that the interaction of relief and pattern, which is so easily produced by vacuum or pressure forming, offers wide possibilities. Of course the image distorts, but, with careful design, this can be used to effect.

The problems of post forming are few providing the correct inks have been used; if the plastics has accepted the image, it generally survives the forming process. However deep draws can cause the printed areas to break up and show 'stretch' patterns.

Cubic construction in decorated sheet plastics: *Kroa A* by Vasarely. *Photo: Galerie Denise René, Paris.*

If repeated formings are being made of one image, they can easily be changed at will to male or female by alternating the side of the sheet facing the mould.

ANTI-STATIC TREATMENTS

The high resistivity of plastics is an advantage when they are used as electrical insulators, but it also leads to high static charges which attract dirt and dust. On some flat surfaces it is possible for the dirt layer to follow the 'pattern' of the charge, which makes it even more obvious. Any attempt to remove it by normal wiping tends only to move it about the surface and to intensify yet further the static charge.

So far as most workshop activities are concerned, static will only be a problem when handling sheet or film. The

Disposable tableware designed and made at West Surrey College of Art and Design.

hygroscopic, lowers surface resistivity and allows a slow discharge to take place.

Proprietary anti-static agents work in a variety of ways and are available mainly as lacquers for spray and dip coating or impregnated in cloths.

METALLIZING

Vacuum metallizing is essentially an industrial process: it consists of evaporating a metal — usually aluminium — and allowing it to fall on the plastics article in a vacuum. The mirror-like finishes associated with the process are made possible by first lacquering the article to obtain a perfect surface. It is usual to stove this coating before metallizing. As the deposition takes place in a vacuum, the particles travel in straight lines and, unless the article is rotated, some areas would be masked and thus look 'starved'.

It is possible to mask out areas which are not to be covered.

The amount of metal deposited can be measured in millionths of an inch and thus is not at all resistant to abrasion. It is necessary, therefore, to coat it with a further transparent lacquer which can be tinted to give different effects. A yellow tinted lacquer, for example, gives a gold look.

Transparent materials such as acrylic (polymethyl methacrylate) or polystyrene can be treated on the under surface so that the reflective layer is seen through the material.

The process is not feasible on a small workshop scale, but specialist companies will undertake the treatment to order.

DYEING OF PLASTICS

Not all plastics are receptive to the dyeing process and no hard and fast rules can be given as to which can and which cannot be dyed. Much depends on the composition of the material and the amount of filler or plasticizer it contains. Some can be dyed in certain colours only, some reject dyes completely.

Nylon can be dyed more easily than most plastics, and the small packets of dye which are available commercially can be used for both fibres and mouldings. Moulded polystyrene and some thermosetting plastics are difficult to dye, though expanded polystyrene dyes fairly readily. Data supplied by Messrs. Skilbeck Bros., in Table 11, gives recipes for dyeing various materials. Articles to be dyed should be thoroughly cleaned before dyeing and rinsed afterwards.

charge can build up simply by separating two sheets or by removing a sheet from a mould. Depending on the polarization of the charges, sheets may be difficult to separate or they may repel each other. Thus static can easily build up on production runs, and for this reason most machines are fitted with devices for discharging. Such attachments effectively discharge electricity, but they do not prevent the subsequent build up of further charges. These can best be prevented by using one of the proprietary anti-static agents.

Static builds up easily in a warm dry atmosphere, and a high degree of humidity does tend to prevent it.

One simple way of reducing static is to wash the sheet in thick soapy water and allow it to drain naturally. A thin soap film remains on the surface which, because it is

Chapter 8
Plastisols

PVC in pure form is extremely rigid and is made flexible only by the addition of plasticizers. By varying the quantity of plasticizer, an extraordinary range of flexibilities can be produced. Plastisols are dispersions of vinyl resin in a matched plasticizer which does not dissolve the resin at normal temperatures but undergoes a mutual solvation process on heating. The product is a rubbery textured material, creamy coloured but lending itself to coloration by a wide variety of pigments. Plastisols are tough, chemically resistant, mostly not highly inflammable and used industrially to produce such goods as soft dolls, industrial gloves, handlebar grips etc. As PVC (polyvinyl chloride) degrades easily when heated, stabilizers are necessary and fillers may also be added to impart other special properties.

The process of gelation is physical rather than chemical and takes place at average temperatures of 150°C—165°C when the change in state is usually rapid.

Handgrip dip moulded by Plastic Coatings Ltd. from PVC material based on BP Chemicals Breon.

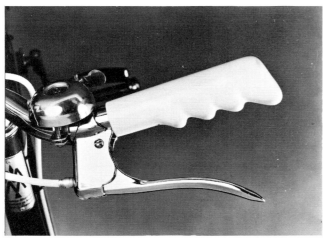

Plastisols are used in the following production processes:
1. CELLULAR AND FOAMED PVC PRODUCTS
2. COATING   (a) Hot dip coating
                (b) Cold dip coating
                (c) Spraying
                (d) Spreading on fabrics and other surfaces
3. MOULDING (a) Slush moulding
                (b) Rotation moulding
                (c) Dip moulding
4. FLEXIBLE MOULDING COMPOUNDS

HOT DIPPING

This is the common industrial technique for the production of such goods as kitchen gloves. In most cases, all aluminium male moulds matching the inner surfaces of the articles being produced are used.

The mould is heated in an oven to pre-gelation temperatures (about 110°C) and then immersed to the required depth in the liquid plastisol. The plastisol begins to solidify as a coating around the form, and when the required thickness is built up, it is slowly withdrawn and inverted so that the inevitable last drip is able to flow out. A coating of up to 3mm is possible in one dip, greater thicknesses necessitating further dipping. After dipping, the form is transferred to an oven set to maintain the curing temperature of the plastics, and, when finally cured, is withdrawn and force cooled by immersion in water until it is at about 60°C—80°C. At this temperature, the plastics can be removed because it is still very flexible, but it is not so soft as to suffer permanent deformation if stretched.

It is common practice to make an air passage through the mould leading to a small hole venting on to the surface at an extremity. By applying air to this, the moulding can easily be blown off. Alternatively, a flattened tube connected to an air line can be inserted beneath the lip of the moulding to similar effect. If the mould is pre-dipped in silicone, release is assisted.

Double dipping should not be carried out over plastics which has completely cured; there is a danger of poor adhesion and subsequent peeling of the top coat. Before the true gelation stage is reached, the paste solidifies somewhat but does not yet possess its properly cured properties. It is at this stage that double dipping should take place. All layers will gel together if they are heated

Opposite and overleaf: Polystyrene sheet engraved with a stylus, painted and postformed in relief by J. Haydon Williams.

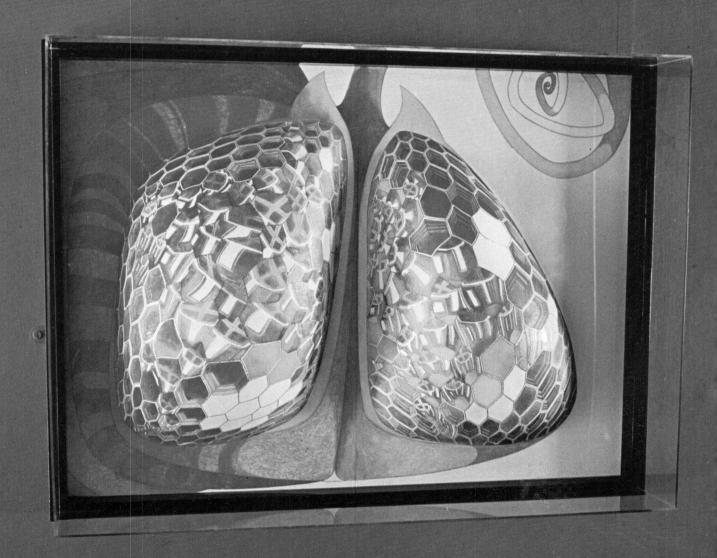

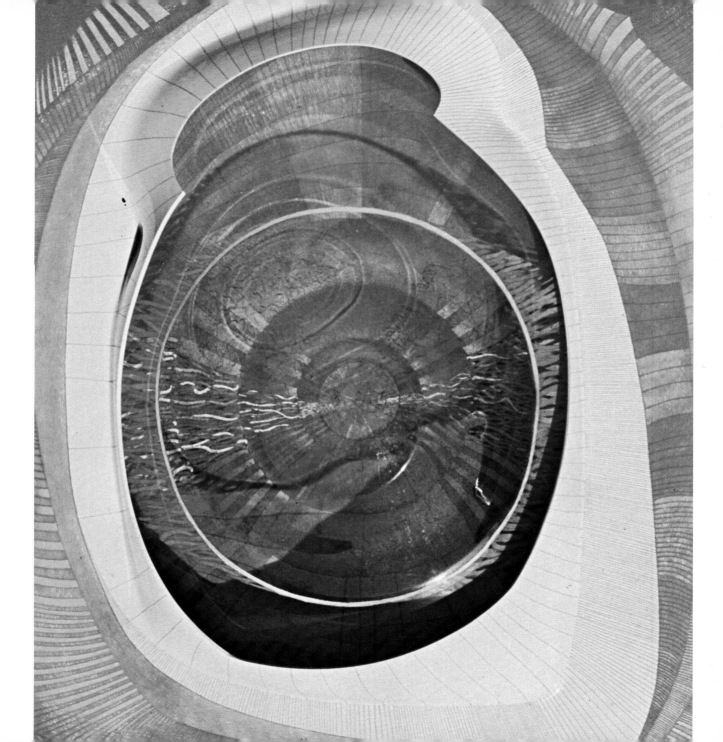

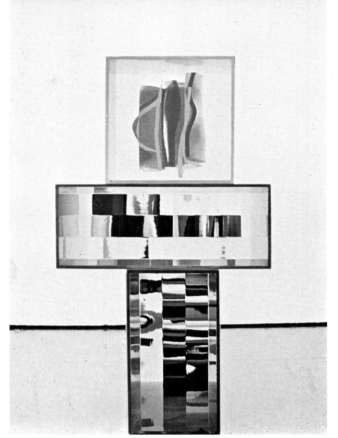

Above: Mural in acrylic by C. A. Meredith.

Above right and right: Works in acrylic material by Michael Dillon.

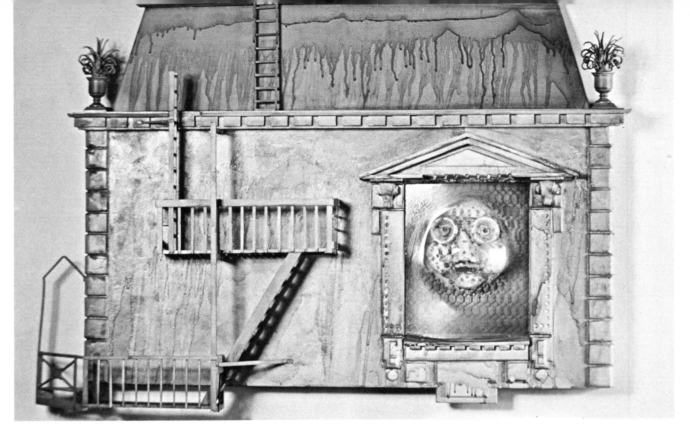

Sculptures from polystyrene sheet worked with a hand torch.
F. Newton.

Dip moulding at Plastic Coatings Ltd.: Glo-cone road warning signs. The coloured tip is applied by second dipping. *Photo: Imperial Tobacco Group Ltd.*

properly in the final stage, but the *true* gelation temperature must be attained. Prolonged heating at only slightly lower temperatures achieves nothing and overheating rapidly degrades the material.

Factors governing the thickness of plastics are:
  (a) The viscosity of the paste
  (b) Heating cycle times
  (c) Temperature of the mould
  (d) Heat capacity of the mould
  (e) General shape of the mould

Quite complex forms can be produced: if they are removed at the correct temperature, forms with undercuts and recesses can be moulded.

A simple coated moulding lacks stiffness, but strengthening webs across the mould are produced by making saw cuts where they are needed. Provided the cuts are not more than $\frac{3}{32}$'' wide, no corresponding depression will be visible on the surface.

Given that an oven is available (a domestic cooker will suffice), these processes can be carried out with little difficulty, the only extra required being a suitable tank for the paste. Moulds are best mounted on a plate with handles as in Diagram 25, because they go in and out of the oven several times per cycle.

Heating and dipping periods are not critical and are best discovered by experiment.

In some cases, materials manufacturers have ceased supplying made up pastes; they supply to converters who make up their own dispersions. In case of difficulty, supplies can usually be obtained from specialist plastics dipping companies.

COLD DIPPING

This is a similar process, mainly used to coat moulds of uneven thickness. Thick parts of metal moulds have a greater heat capacity and acquire a thicker coating of paste if hot dipped.

A metal mould is cold dipped and withdrawn slowly so that excess paste drains off and an even coating remains. This is transferred to an oven set at gelation temperature and heated until cured. The process results in a thin but

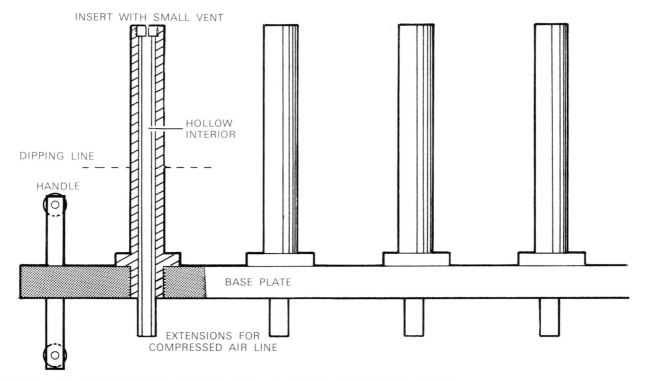

INSERT WITH SMALL VENT

HOLLOW
INTERIOR

DIPPING LINE

HANDLE

BASE PLATE

EXTENSIONS FOR
COMPRESSED AIR LINE

DIAGRAM 25. SIMPLE MOULDS FOR CYLINDRICAL SHAPES SET IN BASE
PLATE FOR HOT DIPPING IN PLASTISOLS

even coating. Greater thicknesses require double dipping.

SPRAYING

Certain types and blends of paste can be sprayed using conventional spray equipment, following which gelation can be achieved in the usual way.

SPREADING

Pastes can be spread over many types of surface: industrially they are applied to wallpapers, fabrics for rain-wear, camping equipment etc. The most common technique is to distribute the paste in an even layer by means of a 'doctor blade' set up as in Diagram 26, the fabric being passed between the blade and a roller covered with a soft blanket. The blade acts like a squeegee, and to contain the paste to the desired area, fences are erected at each end of it. Fabrics are sometimes immersed entirely in paste and then pressed between rollers to remove excess paste.

For small-scale work, the doctor blade principle can be adapted for single surfaces as well as continuous lengths. Hand-held blades (like squeegees) can be filed to an irregular edge and used to produce a variety of relief and combed effects. Different colours can be added locally and many kinds of coarse filler added to give texture.

Embossing Relief patterns are produced in industry by passing the material through cooled embossed rollers at the gelation stage (see Diagram 26). However without such equipment, a variety of relief surfaces can be produced by hand methods. If a cold tool is applied to the paste soon after it is drawn from the oven and held in place until the plastics chills, the impression formed will be permanent. Embossing tools can be made up from printers' rule, or 'found' objects possessing an interesting pattern may be used.

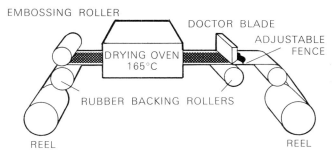

EMBOSSING ROLLER

DOCTOR BLADE

ADJUSTABLE FENCE

DRYING OVEN 165°C

RUBBER BACKING ROLLERS

REEL   REEL

DIAGRAM 26. COATING WITH A DOCTOR BLADE

CASTING PLASTISOLS

Plastisols can be compounded in grades suitable for pouring into hollow moulds. These can be heated to produce 'skin' type mouldings, as in the dipping process, or they can be filled solid. The latter may prove troublesome because very thick sections are difficult to heat thoroughly to achieve true gelation.

A smear of plasticizer over the surface of the mould, particularly over relief parts, helps prevent bubble formation by ensuring that all the surface is 'wetted'.

Open moulds This is the simplest type, similar to a pressed aluminium jelly mould.

Two-part moulds For solid articles, a small orifice should be left through which the plastisol can be injected by a low pressure plunger device, or the mould may be so designed that when the two halves are brought together, excess material is squeezed out. Two-part moulds may also be used for casting a skin on the inside, in which case the process is known as 'slush moulding'.

SLUSH MOULDING

Moulds for this process may be open shells or they may be hollow in two or more parts. They may be fabricated from sheet metal.

The mould is heated to pre-gelation temperature (110°C), filled slowly with paste and allowed to stand while the paste next to the hot face hardens into an interior skin. After about three minutes, when sufficient 'skin' has built up, the excess material is poured off. When the mould has thoroughly drained, it is reheated and kept at gelation temperature until properly cured — usually about twenty minutes. It is then force cooled in water to a convenient temperature for its removal. The process is used in some instances to line vessels with plastics. A sophisticated version of the process, known as 'Rotation Moulding', is described in Chapter 14.

FLEXIBLE MOULDS

Pastes are compounded to serve as hot melt, flexible mould compounds for casting processes in a variety of materials (Vinamould). Manufacturers' instructions should be followed.

NB: the thixotropic consistency of plastisols can be increased by up to 60 per cent where rapid deposition of heavy coatings is required. Proprietary agents are available.

PVC paste does not readily adhere to metal and is only held in place on most coated articles by locking on to surface irregularities or undercuts. Proprietary cements are produced which encourage bonding, and details of these can be obtained from manufacturers.

Chapter 9
Plastics Coating

Plastics coatings are usually applied to metals for protection, typical applications being dish drainers, milk crates, outdoor furniture and industrial components for chemicals. The chief materials employed are polythene (polyethylene), PVC (polyvinyl chloride), CAB (cellulose acetate butyrate) and nylon. The easiest of these to handle is polythene.

An industrial technique adopted for certain materials and applications is to introduce the plastics powder into one of the lines supplying a gas and air torch. The plastics particles are expelled so quickly that they pass through the flame without deterioration. Thus careful application of the flame to the metal surface allows a thickness of plastics to be built up.

However the 'Fluidized Bed' technique is the most commonplace. The object to be coated is pre-heated in an oven to the temperature at which the plastics melts and is then quickly immersed in a bed of finely powdered plastics material. When the powder comes into contact with the heated material, it softens and adheres as a surface coating. This is then returned to the oven for final curing when the surface settles to a glossy finish.

THE FLUIDIZING PRINCIPLE
If compressed air is allowed to enter at the base of the powder and to pass through it, the individual particles of the powder become separated and suspended in the air stream. Thus any object of greater density placed on the top of the mass will sink to the bottom. The principle is known as fluidizing and is essential to the plastics dipping process. Not only does it allow immersion of the object, it also ensures that each part of its surface area is covered with plastics — in the same way that it would be wetted all over if immersed in a liquid.

THE PROCESS
Metal objects require to be thoroughly clean for satisfactory results. Rust, scale and foreign matter should be removed and the object degreased.

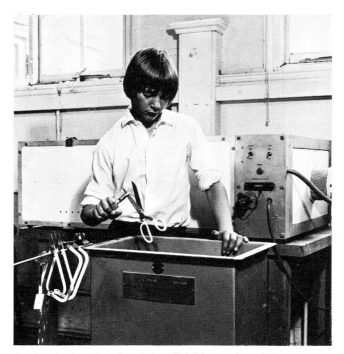

Coating the handles of tools in a fluidizing tank made by Plastic Coatings Ltd. The objects are heated in the home constructed oven to the rear.

If it is to be completely covered, a method must be devised of suspending it in the fluidizing tank and in the oven for curing. If necessary, wire clips can be made up.

The object should be heated in the oven to around the melting point of the plastics chosen. The actual temperature will not only depend on the type of plastics used but also upon the mass of the object. A wire construction will hold less heat than a solid metal one and will consequently need a higher temperature. However 180°C would be a good average.

The article should 'soak' at the correct temperature before it is transferred (usually with tongs) to the fluidizing bed. It is left for some seconds in the powder and withdrawn when the desired thickness has accumulated. On withdrawal, surplus material is tapped off and the object returned to the oven for curing until all the powder which adheres to the surface flows into an even coating.

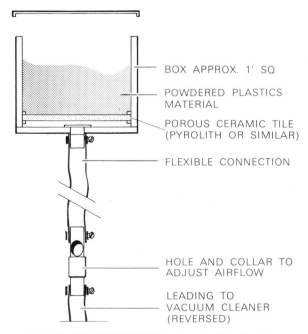

BOX APPROX. 1' SQ

POWDERED PLASTICS MATERIAL

POROUS CERAMIC TILE (PYROLITH OR SIMILAR)

FLEXIBLE CONNECTION

HOLE AND COLLAR TO ADJUST AIRFLOW

LEADING TO VACUUM CLEANER (REVERSED)

DIAGRAM 27. IMPROVISED FLUIDIZING BED

The article can be force cooled by quenching in water, or it may be allowed to cool in air of its own accord. The latter method usually requires some form of support so that the soft coating is not touched.

Where an object has to be totally covered, the defect which remains after the first dipping will require patching. This can often be done by careful work with an open flame. If for any reason the coating is unsatisfactory, it can be burned off with an open flame, but care should be taken to catch molten drips.

MAKING A FLUIDIZING TANK

Diagram 27 shows a typical construction for a fluidizing tank which can operate from a domestic vacuum cleaner. These vary in their output and some experiment may be necessary in selecting the most suitable porous layer. If a ceramic tile is used, an open textured one should be selected. Alternatively, it is possible to use a double layer of canvas.

There should be no air leaks round the porous layer, which should be securely installed.

COATING WITH PTFE

'Non stick' PTFE coatings can be applied to most surfaces which will withstand the high processing temperatures involved — up to 400°C. PTFE is not applied as a powder; it comes as a dispersion in a liquid. This is usually sprayed on to the object, the depth of coating being fairly critical. Normal spray equipment at about 20 lb/in² can be used. Sometimes a primer coat is necessary. The layer is oven dried at about 90°C to evaporate the water and then heated to about 350°C (oven temperature 400°C) at which point a sintering process takes place. That is, the material does not completely flow out but the individual particles fuse together. For general metal applications, Messrs ICI and E.I. du Pont de Nemours & Co. Inc. produce 'Fluon' and 'Teflon' respectively and technical data is available for these materials.

CAUTION Noxious fumes may be given off during the process and if particles are allowed to collect on cigarettes sickness can result. Precautions should be taken and manufacturers will advise on medical aspects.

Coating a piece in a tank made at Lanchester Polytechnic.
Photo: ICI Plastics Division.

Chapter 10
Foams and
Expanded Plastics

FOAMED PLASTICS
Generally these are made by adding a chemical agent to the basic plastics which causes it to foam and expand like soap suds. The effect is produced by the liberation of internal gases during the reaction, and the pressures of these cause the surface of each 'bubble' to link with those of its neighbours. Chemical agents work in various ways. Gases can be produced from the addition of a chemical agent *in situ* as is usual with polyurethanes. Alternatively, they can be produced by the action of a 'blowing agent', as is usual with vinyls, polythenes, and polystyrenes. This is incorporated in the plastics and is designed to decompose and give off nitrogen when a temperature equivalent to the softening point of the plastics is reached.

EXPANDED PLASTICS
These are made by causing solid granules of virgin material to expand. In the case of polystyrene, this is usually achieved by subjecting to steam pressure granules which have been formulated with special solvents. The solvents become vapourized when heated to the temperature at which the plastics softens, and the vapours thus released cause the softened granules to expand.

The process of moulding polystyrene is usually carried out in two stages: the steam process so far described is used to produce pre-expanded granules and final moulding is effected by placing these in a closed mould and subjecting them again to steam pressure. There is sufficient residual action to cause the cells to resoften and expand still further so that they join up and take up the inner form of the mould.

By controlling the size of the cells, various densities are produced for various applications. The very lightest grades are made up of cells up to $\frac{3}{8}''$ in diameter, and these can often be crumbled by the separation of the individual cells. On the other hand, the denser materials are better bonded, much stronger and have a crisper texture. Table 8 shows the comparative densities, softening points, chemical resistance and solvent resistance of common cellular materials.

Closed cell structures are made up of cells which are completely closed off from each other; open cell structures, on the other hand, have cells which are interconnected. For these reasons, open cell structures are generally associated with flexible materials where applications requiring water absorption are common, and closed cell structures are usually found in the rigid forms of the material.

MOULDING EXPANDED POLYSTYRENE
Although mainly used for industrial purposes, the pre-expansion process described can be carried out very simply by passing steam at boiling point through polystyrene beads. A metal box can be improvised for this purpose (Diagram 28) and the steam dispersed through a series of small holes drilled in a non-ferrous tube. (Ferrous metals lead to problems with rust.) To resist condensation, it is a good idea to insulate the box. It is necessary to stir the

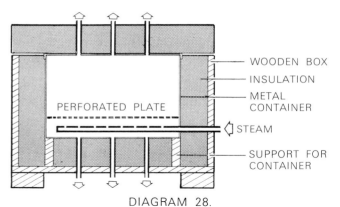

DIAGRAM 28.
EXPANSION CHAMBER FOR POLYSTYRENE

beads several times during processing to ensure that expansion is even.

Moulds for slab-sided articles can be fabricated out of sheet metal with inlets for steam provided all over the surface. A moulding is produced by filling the cavity with pre-expanded beads and subjecting them to further steam pressure. The mould can be force cooled in water.

For experimental pieces, a domestic type of pressure cooker can be used to provide pressurised steam.

HOT WIRE CUTTING
Expanded polystyrene is produced in thin rolls, sheet and

Cutting shapes with the bow cutter.

block form. At relatively low temperatures, the material melts completely, and this, coupled with its low density, allows a suitably heated edge to cut through it very quickly indeed. The cleanest cut is produced with a hot wire; when hot knives are used, the blade following the cutting edge continues heating the sides of the cut so that rough edges due to over-heating tend to occur.

Electrically heated wire cutting tools can be produced in a variety of shapes and sizes.

CAUTION A transformer should always be used to reduce the mains voltage to a safe level. On no account should wire elements be connected to the mains.

HOT WIRE CUTTERS

Simple cutters may be hand held and the wire stretched across a bow as in Diagram 29. These are sometimes made with a pair of wires to enable parallel cuts to be made. A bench type cutter, suitable for a wide range of work, is shown in Diagram 30. Apart from the transformer and electrical components, this can be fabricated entirely in the workshop. The wire can be arranged to cut at an angle in

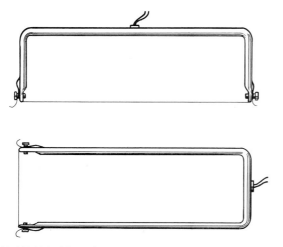

DIAGRAM 29. BOW TYPE HOT WIRE CUTTERS

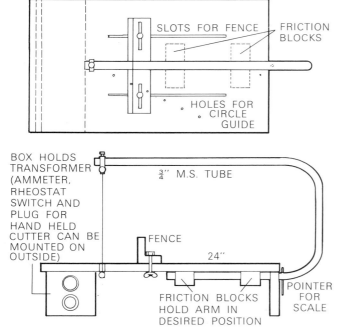

SLOTS FOR FENCE

FRICTION BLOCKS

HOLES FOR CIRCLE GUIDE

BOX HOLDS TRANSFORMER (AMMETER, RHEOSTAT SWITCH AND PLUG FOR HAND HELD CUTTER CAN BE MOUNTED ON OUTSIDE)

¾" M.S. TUBE

FENCE

24"

FRICTION BLOCKS HOLD ARM IN DESIRED POSITION

POINTER FOR SCALE

DIAGRAM 30. HOT WIRE CUTTER FOR POLYSTYRENE

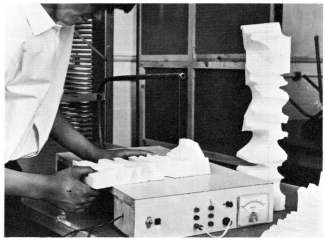

Cutting expanded polystyrene in block form with the table cutter.

two ways; either the top terminal can be made to move along the arm, and the arm marked off with a scale against various angles, or the arm itself can be made to pivot in its fixing underneath the table. If a fence is provided, accurate repetitive cuts can be made. Circular shapes can be cut by placing a point in one of the guide holes and using it as a centre pivot, the distance from the point to the wire being the radius of the circle to be cut.

A typical specification would be nickel chrome wire 32 s.w.g., 11" effective heated length, to operate from a toy train transformer at 12v DC 1½ amps. A motor car battery would also serve.

As hot wire cutters are usually required in various sizes, some advice is given on calculating voltages.

Calculating the voltage and thickness of wire For most practical purposes, the wire selected is likely to be in the range 25–35 s.w.g. (0.20"–0.10"). This combines suitable mechanical strength · with electrical properties. Nickel chrome wire or similar is required and can be purchased in suitable thicknesses in electrical shops. In case of difficulty, spiral elements as produced for electric fires will serve if they are straightened out. The actual temperature of the wire is not critical; it should operate at just under red heat. The required voltage can be read off Diagram 31. For calculation purposes, a wire temperature of around 450°C should be used.

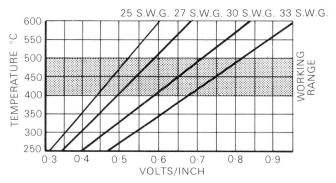

DIAGRAM 31.
TEMPERATURE, VOLTS/INCH, NICKEL CHROME WIRE

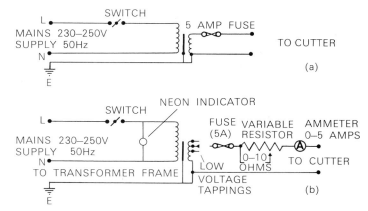

DIAGRAM 32.(a) and (b) CIRCUITS FOR HOT
WIRE CUTTER

WIRE		TEMPERATURE °C		
GAUGE		300	400	500
25 S.W.G.	VOLTS/INCH	0·35	0·43	0·53
	VOLTS/INCH	4·24	5·22	6·36
	VOLTS/CM	0·14	0·17	0·20
27 S.W.G.	VOLTS/INCH	0·39	0·49	0·58
	VOLTS/FOOT	4·72	5·88	7·05
	VOLTS/CM	0·15	0·19	0·23
30 S.W.G.	VOLTS/INCH	0·46	0·58	0·71
	VOLTS/FOOT	5·60	7·00	8·57
	VOLTS/CM	0·18	0·23	0·28
33 S.W.G.	VOLTS/INCH	0·54	0·67	0·82
	VOLTS/FOOT	6·50	8·14	9·85
	VOLTS/CM	0·21	0·27	0·32

Example: required: to make a 12″ cutter using 30 s.w.g. at a temperature of 450°C. From the graph, volts per inch for 30 s.w.g. at 450°C = 0.65 volts/inch. Thus 12 × 0.65 = 7.8 volts.

Allow 20–25 per cent for voltage drop in connecting wires and for adjustments. Transformer output required: 10.0 volts.

When cutting the wire, allow 6″ extra length for setting up purposes.

The following data was obtained using 240v 1000 watt for nickel chrome wire (approximately 27 s.w.g. as used for replacement electric fire elements) on medium density expanded polystyrene.

AC AMPS	VOLTS/ INCH	VOLTS/ FT.	TEMP°C	REMARKS
2.0	0.384	4.60	300	Just cutting
2.5	0.487	5.85	400	Fairly good. Clean cut
3.0	0.590	7.08	500	Clean fast cut
3.5	0.706	8.60	575	Tending to melt surrounding material

Transformer ratings (low voltage current) for temperatures up to 550°C are:

WIRE GAUGE	RATING IN AMPS
25 s.w.g.	4.0
27 s.w.g.	3.5
30 s.w.g.	2.0
33 s.w.g.	1.5–2.0

Basic power supply unit When operating from 240v mains supply, a double wound isolating transformer must be used. The low voltage supply at the exposed element is then entirely safe. Transformers are obtainable with either single or tapped outputs. Typically, the latter will be 12, 15, 20, 25 or 30 volts at 3.0 amps.

Setting up and testing It is not possible to solder nickel chrome wire, so good mechanical joints are essential. A simple circuit is shown in Diagram 32a. When the wire is mounted, a permanent electrical connection can be made at one end, but a temporary connection should be made at the other, leaving an extra length for test purposes. The best position for permanent connection can then be discovered by varying the point of attachment along the free end. If the wire temperature is too low, the effective heated length should be shortened.

Including an ammeter and variable resistor A more sophisticated cutter incorporates an ammeter and variable resistor. The ammeter is particularly useful because it indicates how much current, and hence how much heat, the various densities require.

It is possible to use a motor car battery charger providing the current rating is adhered to and providing it has sufficient voltage, but it should be remembered that normal transformers supply alternating current whereas a battery charger will give a fully rectified current. Thus they will give different ammeter values for a given heat in the cutting wire. Diagram 32b indicates a suitable circuit for the inclusion of an ammeter and variable resistor.

HAND TOOLS

Straight wire cutters are useful for all slabbing types of cuts, but a shaped tool is required for small radiused cuts or for excavating block material.

Hot wires again provide the best cutting edge and they can be bent to any desired shape. A useful selection of shapes is shown in Diagram 33. It is enough to fit such

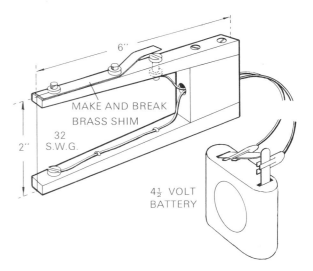

DIAGRAM 34. SMALL HOT WIRE CUTTER

DIAGRAM 33. SHAPES FOR HOT WIRE CUTTERS

wire tools into suitable handles (file handles will do) and heat them over an open flame. If this method is employed, the wire should be reasonably thick — say 12 s.w.g. — so that it holds sufficient heat to complete the cut. Alternatively, the wire can be electrically heated by connecting to a transformer as previously described.

For schools or for very light work, a small battery operated cutter can be made as in Diagram 34. If 32 gauge wire is used, it can be operated from a 4½v battery.

Injecting polyurethane foam for insulation.
Photo: BP Chemicals.

Left: Using the small hot wire cutter described.

POLYURETHANE FOAM

This is the material most commonly used for *in situ* foam forming. It is obtainable as a two-part liquid pack containing components A and B. These, when mixed together, produce foamed polyurethane. The density can be altered by varying the proportions of the two components and flexible or rigid types can be produced.

The material is used industrially for buoyancy fillers, as insulation, and, in flexible form, as an upholstery material. Crash paddings for motor cars are often made by foam filling a preformed PVC skin.

It is useful to note that, unlike polystyrene, it is not dissolved by polyester resin and consequently can be used as a core material for GRP work.

The material is simple to use providing the manufacturers' instructions are followed.

PROJECTS IN CELLULAR PLASTICS

Relief panels Polystyrene is easily worked into relief patterns: everyday metal objects — tube, section, nuts, bolts and so on — can be heated and lightly impressed to form a pattern. It is a good idea to spend some time making a collection of such objects so that a variety of impressions can be produced. Objects to be impressed can be heated in an open flame; the degree of heating is not critical. Panels worked in this fashion can be coloured or inlaid, or they can serve as a mould for casting in another material.

Casting from polystyrene Castings from polystyrene can be taken in most materials, though it should be noted particularly that polyester resins (as used for GRP work) act as very strong solvents.

When casting from concrete, no release agent is necessary. After the concrete has set, the bulk of the polystyrene can be pulled away and the residue adhering to the surface removed with a blow-lamp.

Metal casting Expanded polystyrene can be sculpted into forms by any of the methods described, and from these

Left: Sculptural rainwater duct for the Town Hall, Guildford, carried out by students of West Surrey College of Art and Design. Wooden shuttering was lined with expanded polystyrene in which the relief image was made with hot tools.

Above: Shows the concrete being poured.

Opposite: Coalville Grammar School Leics.: mural in cast concrete from expanded polystyrene shutter linings. Designed by Anthony Hollaway.

forms metal castings can easily be produced. For 'one off' castings, the EPS can be embedded direct in casting sand with the usual runners, feeders and vents leading from it. When the hot metal is poured, the EPS (expanded polystyrene) immediately burns away leaving no trace on the casting.

Colouring EPS can be coloured by many types of paint, but cellulose-based paints are particularly strong solvents and cannot be used. For general purposes, emulsion paints are most suitable. Oil-based paints can have a softening effect and should not be used, although certain enamels and Chinese lacquer are quite suitable. The material may be dyed to the recipe given in Table 11.

PART 3
POLYESTER
RESINS

Chapter 11
Glass Reinforced
Polyesters

GENERAL

The process consists of lining a mould with a layer of acti-vated liquid resin into which strands of glass-fibre are embedded so that, on hardening, the laminate so formed can be withdrawn from the mould. Epoxy and polyester resins are used, although epoxy, being more expensive, is only used where its inherent characteristics are essential. Polyester resins are sometimes known as 'Fibreglass resins'* and this chapter is concerned with these.

The base resin comes in a liquid form, usually a solution of polyester in the monomer styrene. It is the styrene com-ponent which gives the base product its potential to develop a cross-linked molecular structure, thus preventing the material from being resoftened to the plastic state.

CATALYSTS AND ACCELERATORS

Polyester resins are not stable; left on their own they undergo partial gelation – though this does take many months. To induce the resin to harden, it is necessary to add a catalyst. The catalyst is the essential component which starts and maintains the setting process, but when added on its own, the gelation period is still slow, though at higher tempera-tures the process speeds up considerably. To bring gelation time to more reasonable working limits, an accelerator is added, and this, depending on quantity and formulation, can reduce gelation time to a matter of minutes. Nowadays it is possible to purchase base resins which already contain the accelerator and these only need a catalyst added.

CAUTION These materials are unstable. See page 79 for precautions which must be observed.

THE GELATION AND CURING PROCESS

Hardening commences as soon as the catalyst has been added, and the process is exothermic. In extreme conditions a plain unfilled mix with ample additives can reach tempera-tures of 140°C–150°C.

The first stage in the setting process takes place after

*Fibreglass is a trademark of Fibreglass Ltd.

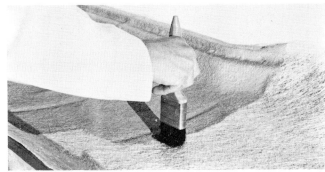

The contact moulding process:
Above: Application of release agent to the mould surface.
Above right: Application of gel coat.
Right: Impregnation of glass mat with resin.
Below: Typical rollers used to assist impregnation.
Below right: Final moulding and mould.
Photos: Scott Bader.

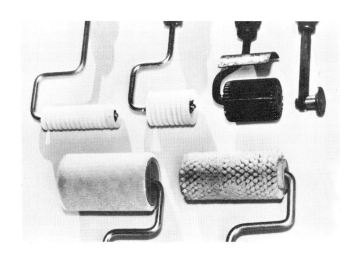

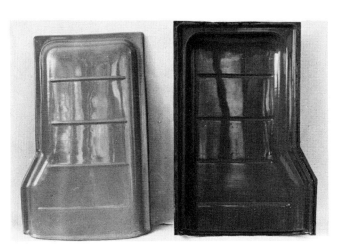

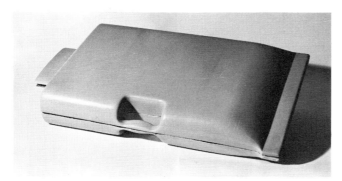

Portable case in GRP for drawing implements by a first-year Foundation course student.

The original pattern and mould.
Photos: West Surrey College of Art & Design.

Sword. This vessel, 64' long, is claimed to be the largest all-GRP production yacht in the world. Designed by J. Hargreaves, moulded by Halmatic Ltd. in Scott Bader Crystic resin.

Sculpture by John Hilliard for City of London Festival.
Photo: Scott Bader.

about twenty minutes when the resin 'goes off', often fairly suddenly, into a jelly-like consistency. After a further thirty minutes or so, the mix is hard enough to handle although at this stage it is not properly cured and may well distort badly if removed from the mould. A period of weeks is usually necessary before the curing process reaches maturity. Gelation and maturing times are mostly governed by the accelerator and catalyst content; gel time will be extended if less catalyst is used. If insufficient catalyst is used, the resultant laminate may be undercured and weak. If less accelerator is used, the gel time will be similarly extended. A large mass of resin will set off faster than a thin layer. Low temperatures inhibit the process and the room temperature should not fall below 15°C. The glass fibre itself, like all fillers, has the effect of prolonging gelation.

PIGMENTS AND FILLERS
Polyester resins are transparent but a wide variety of colours can be incorporated into the mix which makes the final moulding self-coloured throughout.

Metallic finishes can be obtained by incorporating metal powders, and mouldings containing these can be polished to give a very convincing metallic effect. Bronze filled resins can even be acid treated to produce a patina. Such fillers are costly, so they are usually only incorporated into the gel coat, the backing laminate being in plain resin. Stone effects can also be obtained by mixing in graded stone dust. A highly reflective 'glitter' surface can be obtained by incorporating tinsel or metal flake, but this should not be mixed in with the resin. A thin layer of gel coat is applied and the metal flake dusted on to this. This is then backed up by further layers.

THE GLASS FIBRE
Glass fibre is made by drawing glass in long filaments of about .0003″ diameter. These are bundled together into strands which can be woven into various thicknesses of glass cloth. They can also be wound together on to a bobbin as a continuous roving or made into glass mat. Mat is not woven; it is made up of short chopped lengths of intermingled strands held together by size.

THE BARRIER FILM OR RELEASING AGENT
To ensure that the moulding parts from the mould with no adhesions, the mould is coated with an inert barrier film called a release agent. Spirit solutions of polyvinyl alcohol are produced commercially for this purpose. Wax polishes can be used, though those which contain silicones often cause adhesions due to their tendency to resist wetting by

the resin coating which crawls into globules. Release agents are usually tinted and are available for surfaces with varying porosities.

Care should be taken that there is an adequate and even covering and that no pools have collected in recesses. A new mould should have several coats of wax before the barrier film is applied.

LAYING THE GEL COAT OR SURFACE COAT
The layer of resin first applied to the mould face will be the finished surface of the moulding, so it must be free of blemishes. This 'gel' coat is applied with no glass reinforcement. It provides a certain depth of resin which keeps the glass fibres back in the body of the material where there is less risk of their exposure by abrasion. If uncoated fibres are exposed on the surface, there is risk of water permeation. Colours, where required, are added to the gel coat and should be thoroughly mixed in, otherwise unsightly streaks may appear which can also cause stresses. Stresses can also be set up by uneven coating; thicker parts harden faster which can lead to warping and crazing.

The gel coat should be as thick as a heavy coat of paint, about $\frac{1}{32}$″. If it is too thin, the gelation time may be impaired and the relief image of the glass fibres may appear on the surface. If it is too thick, the surface will be brittle, easily fractured, and may develop deep cracks and crazes.

A thixotropic additive (an agent which increases viscosity) is essential on steep surfaces, but the resin must not be made so thick that it will not flow properly over the release agent.

The gel coat must be allowed to set off somewhat before the laying up proper can begin, although it must not be allowed to cure too far or the next layer may delaminate later on, allowing the surface coat to flake. On the other hand, laying up should not begin until the gel coat is so hard that it cannot be dissolved by the next layer. When the first layer is tacky to the touch but the fingers remain clean, the time is right. Early laying up may cause a relief impression of the glass fibre to show through, or the gel coat may become undulating or wrinkled.

PREPARING THE GLASS MAT
If glass mat sections are cut to shape before the laying up begins, laying up is more leisurely with less risk of contaminating tools and work surfaces. It is convenient to use the weight of the mat to calculate the amount of resin to mix, an average ratio being one of glass to two and a half of resin. Allow that $\frac{1}{16}$″ mat weighs 2 ozs. per sq. ft. Frayed edges tend to release fibres which build up on the brush.

LAYING UP

To measure the catalyst and accelerator, a purpose-made 10cc dispenser is desirable. When these have been added to the resin in proportions recommended by the manufacturer, the mix should be stirred thoroughly — taking care not to introduce bubbles by setting up a vortex.

A fairly thick layer is applied to the gel coat and the mat layed up immediately. This is then 'stippled' until it is saturated. Until now the mat has been held together by its binder, but this now dissolves so that the fibres are free in suspension. This causes the mat to 'soften' sufficiently to follow mould contours. It is essential that the whole surface is covered; dry spots become air bubbles. A second layer can be applied as soon as the first has been thoroughly impregnated. Various rollers are available for assisting the impregnation of larger surfaces. If a smooth surface is required, this can be achieved by laying up progressively finer materials ending in a layer of tissue paper.

Mouldings should not be removed for twenty-four hours. Ragged edges are best trimmed in the 'green' or semi-hard state.

Heating up to 60°C may accelerate the curing, but as it is difficult for the heat to reach the important surface, the gel coat, there is a danger that the curing of this may be comparatively retarded.

REINFORCING

Large GRP mouldings, because they are a simple shell form, tend to flex easily and may need stiffening. This can be achieved by thickening the edges and applying box sections to the back surface. This can be achieved by laminating over any suitable hollow section, though reinforcements of this type should not be made while the moulding is soft, otherwise contractions will cause distortions. The removal of the laminate from the mould can sometimes present problems, especially when the moulding will not flex. Where possible, edges should be eased away, and a jet of compressed air between surfaces which have been so freed will often extend separation and cause release. A compressed air line can be incorporated in the mould leading to the interface, so that the moulding can be blown off. Where painting is required, care must be taken that all traces of wax and release agent have been removed, and it is a good idea to sand the surface to provide a key.

The most common fault is the breaking up of the surface into fissures called crazing. It is usually found in areas of concentrated resin with little reinforcement, or it may be due to using the wrong resin or resin mix.

Above: Preparing a pigmented polyester resin mural for Abbeywood School, London. Anthony Hollaway.

Opposite: Decorative panels in polyester, designed and made by N. March.

The need for organization It is necessary to be scrupulously clean and methodical otherwise tools, work surfaces and even the operator himself become covered in a layer of sticky resin. Brushes and tools should be cleaned in acetone before hardening begins.

CAUTION Catalysts are unstable, so they are normally supplied as dispersions in a paste or liquid plasticizer. Accelerators are usually based on cobalt. These two substances should never be mixed together directly; the resultant reaction could be explosive. For this reason also, they they should be kept separate for storage and waste disposal, and fire precautions for peroxide-based materials observed.

People who are sensitive to irritation by the glass fibres should wear gloves to protect the skin from penetration by the fibres. Barrier creams should also be used. The work space should be well ventilated.

If any GRP material enters the eyes, they snould be washed with a weak solution of sodium bicarbonate and a doctor informed.

Mural in the Banking Hall of Lloyds Bank, Eastbourne. GRP with inserts of stainless steel. Designed by Anthony Hollaway.

Chapter 12
Casting, Embedding and
Simple Polyester Techniques

MOULDS
Moulds can be made out of GRP (glass reinforced plastics) from a pattern made in any modelling material — clay, plaster, wax, wood, etc. A simple one-piece mould can be made over a clay pattern modelled on a sheet of glass. Resin and glass mat is laid up over the pattern as described in Chapter II until a thick rigid layer is built up. This must be thick to withstand rough handling and to prevent warping.

Two-part moulds (**Diagram 35**) The pattern must be so designed that the two mould halves can withdraw from a parting line. It is crucial that the parting line is accurately traced. The model is then embedded in clay, up to and accurately following the parting line, and the first half laid up. (See Diagrams 35a and b.) When the resin has cured, the work is inverted, the clay 'fencing' pulled away and the second half laid up. (See Diagrams 35c and d.) When both halves have thoroughly cured, the mould is split, the model withdrawn, and after cleaning up the mould is ready for laying up. Lay-ups are made in each half and the edges trimmed while soft. The two halves can be joined in the mould or withdrawn and taped together. In either case, the join proper is made by covering with resin-impregnated glass tape.

Flexible moulds Shapes which are complex or with under-cuts are best made in flexible moulds of silicone rubber-based material (Silcoset) or PVC-based material (Vina-mould). Vinamould compounds only become fluid when heated and have to be poured when hot. Models must therefore stand the temperatures involved (120°C to 170°C depending on grade). Silcoset compounds come as liquids or pastes and set solid when activated by the addition of a curing agent. No release agent is necessary with either material when taking GRP casts.

USING FOAMS WITH POLYESTERS
Casting by dissolving expanded polystyrene Polyester resins are strong solvents of expanded polystyrene and this

Trophy for the Welsh Grand National by Adrian Dartnall, third-year student at West Surrey College of Art and Design. A silver saddle form is embedded in perspex. *Photo: Chepstow Racecourse.*

factor can be used to advantage in casting. A model is made up out of expanded polystyrene and an extension, which will be the pouring runner, of about ¾" diameter is added to the base. This is sandpapered to a good finish and given several coats of emulsion paint which serve as a barrier against the resin. The emulsion paint, in turn, is treated with a release agent and a two-part mould made in GRP. The

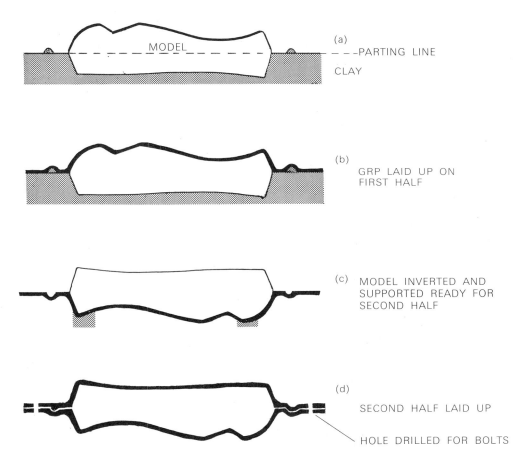

(a) — PARTING LINE

MODEL

CLAY

(b) GRP LAID UP ON FIRST HALF

(c) MODEL INVERTED AND SUPPORTED READY FOR SECOND HALF

(d) SECOND HALF LAID UP

HOLE DRILLED FOR BOLTS

DIAGRAM 35. MAKING A TWO PART GRP MOULD

expanded polystyrene is exposed at the runner so that, when the resin is poured in, it immediately dissolves and allows the resin to take up its place inside the mould.

Because of the risk of cracking (see under Embedding), mouldings of small diameter only should be attempted and casting grade resins employed for filling the mould. Fillers may be incorporated.

Polyurethane foam: this is not attacked by polyester resins and can be shaped into a core for surfacing with GRP. By these means, such articles as surf boards are produced.

Phenolic type foams: these are not attacked by polyesters,

but as the cells are interconnected, a sealant against penetration is necessary.

Expanded PVC: unplasticized PVC is not attacked, but the plasticized varieties may be affected after a period and so a barrier is recommended.

EMBEDDING WITH POLYESTERS

Polyester resins are produced in a wide variety of grades and types ranging from flexible to rigid, transparent to opaque, and a resin suitable for thin sections is not suitable for casting in thick slabs.

The main difficulty encountered in casting large blocks is that they tend to crack up. For this reason, manufacturers have devised special grades of resin which minimize the risk. They are also made in transparent grades, and for embedding purposes these are desirable.

The usual technique for casting large blocks is to build up layers of up to $\frac{1}{2}''$ at a time. While this obviates cracking, the joints between pourings may be visible when the block is viewed end on due to optical distortion.

The layer technique can be used to 'scatter' components within a block; as the block is built up in successive pourings, parts are laid out on the separate layers. (See Diagram 36.)

Ceramic or glass containers make excellent moulds because they produce a glossy surface and do not require release agents. Cylindrical castings may be made inside PVC tubing.

Decorative effects can be obtained by embedding reflective surfaces such as sequins.

NB: the greater transparency and optical properties of acrylics give better results than polyesters, but the technique is not so simple. Specialist firms undertake acrylic embedding and, for one or two off, it is cheaper and easier to use their services. The monomer methyl methacrylate is usually employed. It is catalysed immediately before pouring with a peroxide, but large blocks must still be built up in layers. Various proprietary materials are available for embedding with acrylic and the manufacturers' instructions should be followed.

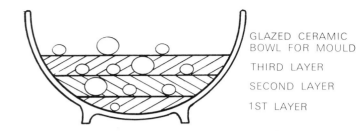

GLAZED CERAMIC
BOWL FOR MOULD

THIRD LAYER

SECOND LAYER

1ST LAYER

DIAGRAM 36. EMBEDDING

RELIEF COPYING

Where it is not possible to lay up directly on to a relief surface, it is often possible to make the impression first in a soft foil such as aluminium cooking foil, and then to cast the resin into this foil. The foil is taped over the relief and 'stippled' into the surface with a dry brush. The impressed foil is then mounted on a backing board and resin laid into it.

Opposite upper: Modelling a relief pattern in clay, utilizing 'found' objects to impress the pattern.

Opposite lower: Pouring the polyester resin.

FILAMENT WINDING HOLLOW WARE

The technique provides for a continuous filament of glass fibre to be wound around a cylindrical mould. A slight taper is necessary on the mould to allow the release of the moulding or, alternatively, disposable moulds of, say, PVC tubing may be used. Polythene containers may also be improvised. The mould is mounted in a frame with provision to rotate it, and the rovings are likewise mounted on a roller opposite (see Diagram 37).

A release agent may be used, or polyester film or scotch tape wound on to the former. A gel is applied in the normal way and the filament wound on to this layer. Different coloured resins may be used on the same winding. The filaments should intersect on the former at wide angles to assist longitudinal strength. They should not be wound on in 'cotton reel' fashion.

The technique is popularly used for making lamp shades, bins etc. Forms which narrow in the middle can be made up over two parts which withdraw at either end.

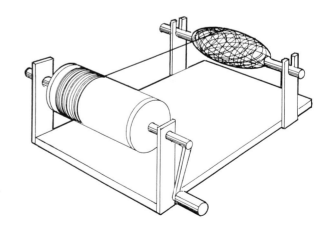

DIAGRAM 37. FILAMENT WINDING GRP

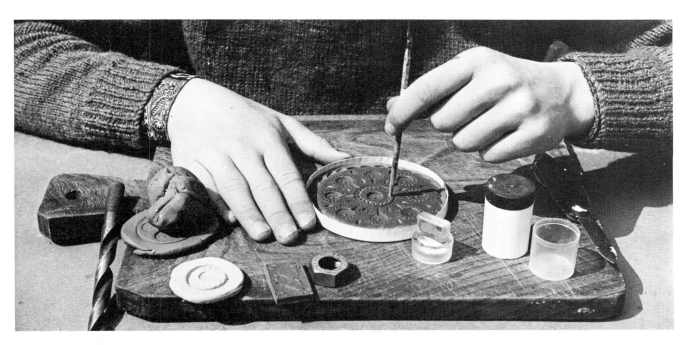

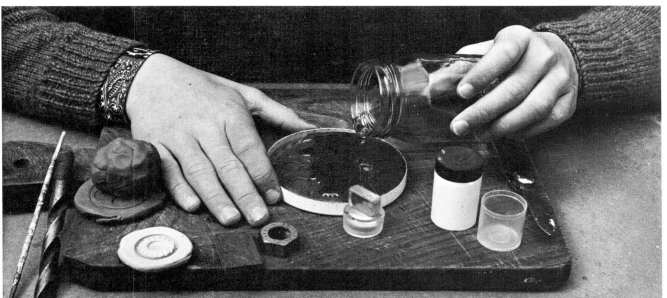

DECORATIVE TRANSPARENT PANELS

By pouring casting grade resins on to a glass surface, a highly polished flat moulding is produced. The back surface can also be given an improved surface by stretching a film of polythene or cellophane over it. This will release easily when the resin has cured.

It is necessary to erect fences of clay on the edges to retain the layer, and, of course, the surface must be quite level. The thickness should not exceed $\frac{1}{4}''$. Different coloured resins may be used, and if different coloured tissues are embedded, controlled shapes can be achieved. If the resin is laid up on to an embossed glass, particularly one with a geometric pattern, further interest is created.

Relief panels can be cast from thick polythene sheet,

where the design has been engraved with lino-cutting tools. The incised lines will be raised on the moulding and the spaces between, or 'fields', can in turn be filled with coloured resins.

ODDMENTS OF RESIN

Resin leftovers can be poured into suitable shapes for conversion into jewellery etc. If odd colours are poured into PVC tubing, variegated rods are produced which may be converted to pendants or cut into discs and drilled to make rings. Brooch pins can be set into the resin.

Small reliefs can be cast from wax. The wax is melted in a tin lid and allowed to cool so that it sets. A design is engraved or impressed on this, and it appears as an embossed image when a resin cast is taken.

Left: Acrylic block by Stanley Plastics Ltd.

Opposite: Engineering components embedded for display
purposes. Stanley Plastics Ltd.

PART 4
INDUSTRIAL
PROCESSES

Chapter 13
Vacuum Forming

Vacuum forming is not a single process, it is the term applied to a range of techniques which utilize atmospheric pressure to secure contact between a heated sheet of plastics and a mould. In Chapter 5 various vacuum and compressed air assisted techniques were described, but in this chapter the more sophisticated techniques of vacuum forming proper are covered.

A basic vacuum former consists of a frame and clamp which holds a plastics sheet in airtight contact over a box which is itself airtight. The box is connected to a vacuum pump. Over the frame is a movable set of heaters. The essential sequence of operations is as follows (see Diagram 38):

(1) A mould is placed inside the box.
(2) The plastics material is clamped in the frame over the box so that it is airtight.
(3) Heaters are brought over the plastics and removed when it has softened.
(4) The plastics is brought into contact with the mould and the vacuum applied until the plastics takes up the form of the mould under atmospheric pressure.
(5) The plastics is cooled, removed from the mould and excess material trimmed off.

The various techniques are described as female forming, male forming, drape forming, pre-inflated forming, and plug assisted forming. Their advantages and disadvantages are as follows.

Female forming (**Diagram 38a and b**) In this case the plastics is formed inside a concave mould. Very simple equipment can be used. Multi-impression moulds can be close packed without webbing, but the depth of draw is limited and thinning of the walls will arise if deep or extreme contours are attempted.

Male forming This is similar to female moulding except that the mould is convex and the plastics is formed *over* it. The method has the advantage of increased depth of draw, but webbing is more likely to occur.

Drape forming (**Diagram 38e and f**) More sophisticated

Heated plastics sheet ready for the forming process.
Photo: Parnall and Sons, Bristol.

equipment is necessary for this process, since a lifting platform for the mould is required. This allows the mould to be raised up and pushed into the softened plastics material (Diagram 38f), which has the effect of pre-stretching or draping the plastics into the form of the mould before the vacuum is applied. This reduces thinning on deep drawn mouldings so that deeper articles can be produced or a thinner grade of plastics used. The majority of commercial vacuum forming is done in this way. When moulds present special problems of local thinning on deep draws or corners, pre-stretching techniques (pre-inflation or plug assisting) may be necessary.

Pre-inflation When a deep male mould is employed, it is usual to introduce compressed air into the box so that the sheet of plastics is inflated from below into a dome (Diagram 39b). By this method a large area of material is pre-stretched and distributed evenly over the mould. There is also less risk of blemishes due to 'dragging' on the mould.

(a) and (b) FEMALE FORMING

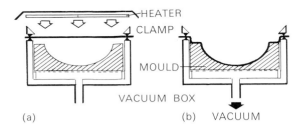

(c) and (d) MALE FORMING

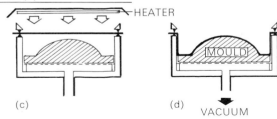

(e) and (f) DRAPE FORMING

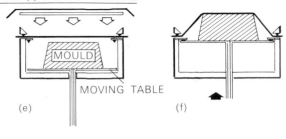

DIAGRAM 38.

(a) HEATING   (b) PRE-INFLATION

(c) MOULD RAISED   (d) VACUUM APPLIED

(e) HEATING   (f) PLUG INSERTED

(g) VACUUM APPLIED

DIAGRAM 39. (a) (b) (c) (d) PRE-INFLATION FORMING
(e) (f) (g) PLUG ASSISTED FORMING

Plug-assisted forming (Diagram 39e–g) Where a deep drawn forming is required in a female mould, the material may be locally stretched with a 'plug' as in Diagram 39f. The object is to carry as much material as possible into the cavity before the vacuum is applied. The plug should be about one-fifth smaller than the female cavity.

DESIGN CONSIDERATIONS

Moulds For small runs, moulds can be of any material which withstands the heat and pressure involved: wood, glass reinforced plastics, epoxy resin, plaster etc. For large runs, they are generally made of metal or metal filled epoxy resin.

No undercuts are permissible, otherwise it would not be possible to withdraw the plastics; there must be taper on all verticals. Sharp edges and corners make for thinning and weak mouldings. The mould must be so shaped that when the plastics is brought into contact, every recess remains connected to the vacuum and no air pockets are trapped. This may require recesses to be drilled to connect to the vacuum. In order that such holes should not leave blemishes, they should be made small and lead into larger holes drilled from the reverse side.

To avoid a radius at the very edge of a forming, it is advisable to surround the outline of the mould with a ring of holes in the base-board. The mould surface should be well finished to facilitate removal of the formed sheet.

Obtaining mouldings of even thickness The disadvantage of the system is that the sheet plastics stretches into unequal thicknesses as it is drawn on to the mould. Where it is most stretched it is weak and thin, and, unfortunately, it usually happens that mouldings are weak where they need to be strong and vice versa. It is the vertical surfaces which thin the most, and this must be accommodated in mould design.

Avoiding 'webbing' 'Webs' are formed where there is an excess of material over a surface or where a peculiarity of the mould, such as a corner or a sharp radius, induces a fold. In either case, as the vacuum is applied, the folded material is drawn together into a 'web'. The risk is increased if (a) it is attempted to form a small object in a large sheet; (b) in multi-impression moulds, the arrangement of individual moulds is too close or the peculiarities of the contours make it unsuitable; (c) the sheet has not been sufficiently softened; (d) the mould has not been properly vented. It can often be obviated on corners by placing a spare vertical block at right angles to the line of the web, thus taking up some of the spare material.

Pinholes and small surface eruptions, usually coupled with discolouration, indicate that the plastics is being overheated.

KEY TO DIAGRAM 40

A Heaters mounted over expanded metal.
B De Sta Co hold down clamps, or similar.
C Angle iron runners for heaters which move on pulley wheels – D.
D Pulley wheels.
E Handle.
F Clamping frame.
G Clamping frame counterweight.
H Pivot for clamping frame, preferably spring loaded.
I Motor and pump.
J Vacuum cylinder.
K Metal tube to lift table. (Sealed at lower end.)
L Supports for lifting tube.
M Perforated metal over table.
N Seals.
O Air cocks, one for vacuum and one for compressed air.
P Lifting pedal, preferably fitted with stop to support table in upper position.
Q Control panel providing mounting for clockwork timer, ON/OFF warning light, air cocks for vacuum and compressed air, ON/OFF switch for heaters, ON/OFF switch for vacuum pump.

BUILDING A VACUUM FORMER

Diagram 40 shows the general arrangement of a vacuum former suitable for home construction, and the following are the main design considerations.

Heaters The aim should be to attain an even heat all over the surface of the plastics. An even radiation pattern can be achieved if a sheet of expanded metal is placed between the elements and the plastics. Polished aluminium reflectors should be fitted above the heaters.

To check that there are no hot or cold spots in the heated area, it is a good idea to experiment with Tempilstiks crayons or Thermindex paints. These are made in various grades and record temperatures either by melting or changing colour. If these are applied to a sheet of metal and the heater bank offered up, any temperature irregularities are immediately evident. A sheet of newsprint placed under the heaters will also show up hot spots by premature browning. The elements may require rearrangement before an even heating effect is obtained.

Elements should be of the black heat type and sheathed. Manufacturers produce these in a wide range of shapes and ratings with various terminals, or they will supply them bent to a pattern. They will recommend a suitable element if they are told (a) the area to be heated, (b) typical materials to be heated, (c) temperature required, (d) nominal distance of heaters from surface, (e) nominal time required to obtain

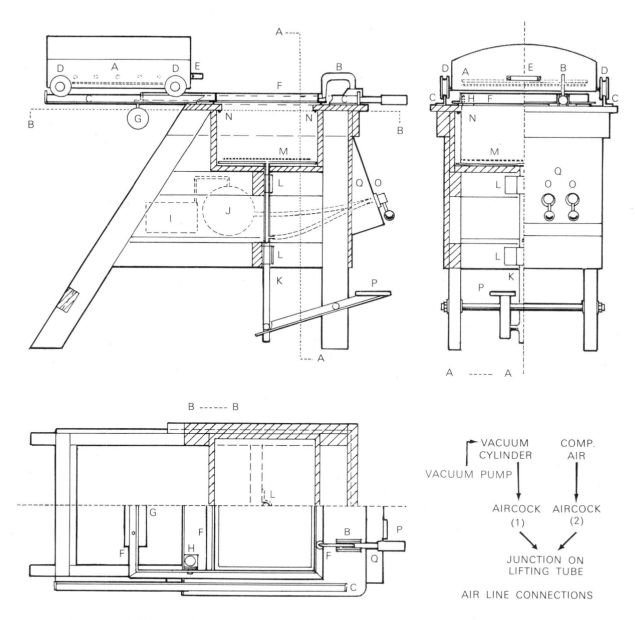

DIAGRAM 40. TYPICAL LAYOUT FOR VACUUM FORMER

AIR LINE CONNECTIONS

Decorative panels, printed and vacuum formed in sheet polystyrene.

temperature, and (f) electricity supply available. It is usual to specify the effective heated length plus any additional length to reach from the heated part to the terminal connection.

There is no fixed time for heating sheet plastics: heat travels by radiation; when it meets the sheet it is either reflected, or it passes through (transmitted), or it is absorbed by the plastics. It is the latter which causes the temperature of the sheet to be raised, and the time this takes varies with such factors as transparency, colour, reflectivity, thickness etc. It follows that there is no single recommended heater loading for a given area, but a general all-purpose figure would be 1kw to 1.5kw per square foot. Plastics sheet manufacturers will always recommend the appropriate loading per unit area for their materials.

Frame construction So long as the frame is robust, it can be made from wood or metal. The top should be of non-combustible material and should be quite flat. The clamping frame should be rigid and warp free. It should also match

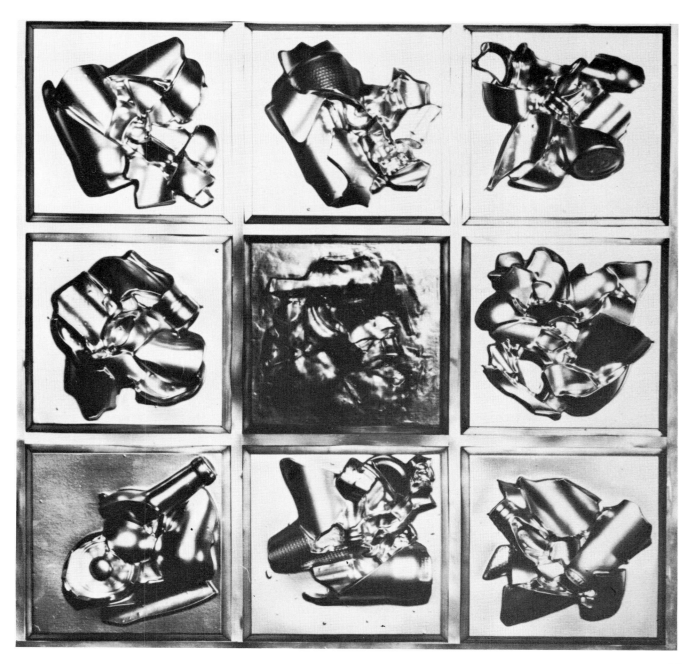

91

the top accurately so that the plastics sheet is gripped evenly all round. A counterweight is not essential but is highly desirable. It is preferable that the hinge blocks for the clamping frame should be spring loaded (Diagram 41) so that a variety of thicknesses can be accommodated. Alternatively, these have to be adjusted with shims, which is time consuming. The clamp itself must be positive and quick acting. Cam types can be used, though the simplest is a toggle type such as the De-sta-co hold down variety.

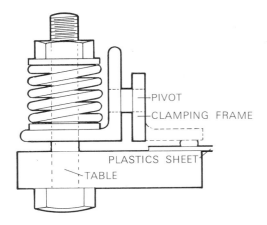

DIAGRAM 41. SPRING LOADED PIVOT FOR CLAMPING FRAME

The vacuum chamber should be robustly made, the depth being governed by the draw which is possible in plastics. Diagram 40 shows a method of incorporating a rising table for drape forming. It is advisable to fit this with a means of locking it in the 'up' position. Provision must be made to withdraw the heaters at the end of the heating cycle and, in the example shown, this is achieved by fitting the heater bank with pulleys which run on angle iron guides.

It is usual to mount all controls on a panel so that they are conveniently at hand. These comprise an ON/OFF switch

Opposite: Printed and vacuum formed panel by N. Palmer, second-year student. *Photo: West Surrey College of Art and Design.*

93

Top: Composite table lamps, all components vacuum formed. Designed by C. A. Meredith.

Above: Vacuum formed tray for furniture. Designed and made by pupils of the Sir Frederic Osborn School, Welwyn Garden City. *Photo: Mr. A. Harness.*

Right above: Vacuum formed light fitting by Andreas Vassiliou, second-year student. The photograph shows the measured drawing, original sketch, wooden moulds and the finished lamp. *Photo: West Surrey College of Art and Design.*

Right: Decorative panel by J. H. Williams.

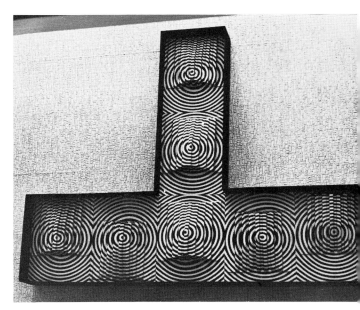

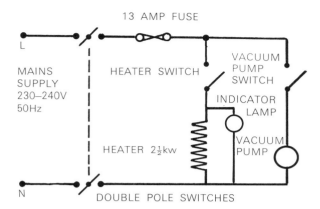

DIAGRAM 42. TYPICAL CIRCUIT FOR
VACUUM FORMER

13 AMP FUSE

L

MAINS
SUPPLY
230–240V
50Hz

HEATER SWITCH

VACUUM
PUMP
SWITCH

INDICATOR
LAMP

HEATER 2½kw

VACUUM
PUMP

N

DOUBLE POLE SWITCHES

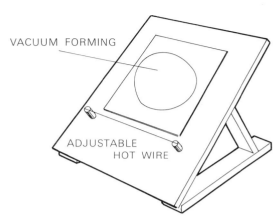

VACUUM FORMING

ADJUSTABLE
HOT WIRE

DIAGRAM 43. TRIMMER FOR VACUUM FORMING

Sledge, vacuum formed in $\frac{3}{16}$" ABS over a wood and resin
mould. Designed by Lunt Usher Design Group, St Albans, Herts.
Reg. Des. No. 956517.

for the pump, an ON/OFF switch for the heaters, one valve
for compressed air, one valve for the vacuum (connected
between the vacuum cylinder and the vacuum chamber)
and a clockwork timer. This is necessary to ensure consistent
cycle times.

The vacuum system As a general guide, the vacuum pump
should be capable of maintaining a pressure differential of
about 25" of mercury in the vacuum chamber. Pump manufacturers will recommend the type necessary to achieve this
against a given volume for the cylinder. They will also
recommend a suitable motor. All air line connections should
be as large a bore as possible to permit sudden evacuation
of the cylinder. There should be no constrictions in the
valves or airways.

Pre-inflated formings can be carried out if a compressed
air line is connected into the chamber via a valve mounted

on the control panel, but the chamber must be capable of
withstanding the pressures without bursting.

CAUTION it is dangerous to connect compressed air lines
to insecure devices. Specialist advice should be sought.

Materials suitable for vacuum forming Most thermoplastics
can be vacuum formed and these are listed in Table 1. The
easiest material is polystyrene, which can be purchased in
a variety of colours and grades. Acrylics (Perspex, Plexiglas)
can be formed over moulds with simple contours but they
do not reproduce detail.

Trimmer for vacuum formings Relief formings can be removed from the sheet with a hot wire cutter as illustrated
in Diagram 43. The sheet should be held in light contact
with the base board to ensure an even depth of cut.

To calculate the loading for the wire, refer to p. 66.

Chapter 14
Industrial Techniques

EXTRUSION

Extrusion is the most widely used industrial process and accounts for a very high percentage of the total volume of plastics produced. Plastics granules are placed in a hopper (Diagram 44) whence they fall into a barrel which is heated

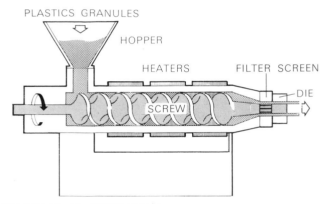

DIAGRAM 44. EXTRUSION

by band heaters from the outside. The plastics melts and is carried along the barrel by a revolving screw to be forced through a die of the required section at the end. Before passing through the die, the spiral movement in the plastics is 'straightened out' and foreign bodies held back by a filter screen.

Dies for tubular sections present a special problem: how to support the mandrel or solid centre section of the mould. The problem is familiar to anyone who has tried to use stencilled letter forms where the middles of the Os readily fall out if severed. In extrusion machines, the problem is overcome by using a 'spider' which joins the mandrel to the outer walls by a series of arms placed so far back in the die that the plastics is able to flow around them. The die is invariably made of substantial heavy steel.

A sophisticated control system regulating temperatures, speeds, pressures etc. is very necessary. These allow infinite lengths of perfectly regular and even section to be consistently produced.

On automatic machines there is usually provision to adjust the size of the section to fairly close tolerances, coupled with a draw off and cooling device. The process is widely adapted for wire coating, in which case the die is basically annular with the wire itself acting as a mandrel being fed in a continuous length through the centre of the die.

Polythene (polyethylene) film may be produced by ex-

Peco 2½'' extruder producing film in tubular form. *Photo: BP Chemicals (UK) Ltd.*

truding a thin walled tube which is immediately further distended by air pressure until the walls are stretched to the required thickness. Infinite lengths of tubing can be produced in this way or, by slitting the sides, film is produced.

BLOW MOULDING

Blow moulding is an immediate post forming extension of the extrusion process. Generally the extruder head and die are turned through 90° to point downwards (Diagram 45). A length of molten tube called a 'parison' is extruded between the two halves of a hollow mould and the mould closed over it. One end of the mould is provided with a 'nip' to seal it off and there is provision at the other to introduce compressed air. This permits the parison to be inflated inside the mould under such pressure that the plastics takes up, fairly accurately, the contours of the mould – rather like

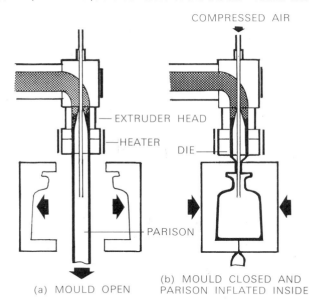

DIAGRAM 45. BLOW MOULDING

blowing up a balloon inside a box.

Moulds are invariably substantially made of heavy steel and may incorporate a water circulating system for cooling.

The process is widely used for containers, bottles and toys.

COMPRESSION MOULDING

This is the simplest form of moulding used for plastics. A split male and female mould is aligned in a press (Diagram 46b) and a measured amount of plastics is placed in the female half of the mould either in granule form or in the form of a prepared tablet. The mould is heated, either by passing steam through cavities or by radio frequency waves, to the softening point of the material being used. When the female tool, which is attached to a plunger, is brought up under great pressure, the softened plastics is forced to take up the impression of the mould. Cold water can be circulated round the cavities of the mould for cooling. The process is invariably applied to thermosetting plastics. The hot press action serves firstly to fill the cavities of the mould and secondly to convert the plastics into a thermo-hardened state. The moulding can be removed, quite stiff and rigid, at not much less than the temperature at which, earlier in the cycle, it flowed into the cavities.

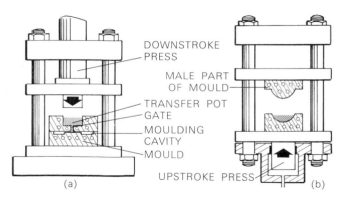

DIAGRAM 46a.
TRANSFER MOULDING

DIAGRAM 46b. COMPRES-SION MOULDING

Although thermoplastics could be formed by this process, it is not used commercially because of the need to cool the mould before the impression can be extracted. In practice, this would result in uneconomic cycle times.

Transfer Moulding

A variation of the simple compression moulding is transfer moulding which allows thicker mouldings, or mouldings with varying thicknesses, to be produced. If variable mouldings are attempted by the ordinary compression process, the thicker sections tend not to be cured in the middle and thin sections tend to be overcured.

In transfer moulding (Diagram 46a) the material is not

Above: Mould and mouldings for use on the small Manumold hand-operated injection moulding machine. *Photo: Messrs. Florin, London.*

Left: Bekum HBV Blow Moulding machine being used by J. Bibby Food Products Ltd. to produce one-litre and half-litre bottles in ICI's Welvic PVC material. Note the pipes taking coolant to the moulds and the parisons being extruded to the rear. *Photo: ICI.*

placed directly in the moulding cavity but in a small 'cylinder' or transfer pot, open to the moulding cavity by a constricted opening known as a gate. The material is evenly preheated in this chamber and, at the appropriate time, a plunger is brought down to force the molten material into the moulding cavity proper.

INJECTION MOULDING

This process has some affinity with die-casting of metals and is universally used for the volume production of solid plastics articles which, because of their shape, can only be moulded. Granules of plastics are heated until they have the consistency of thick toothpaste. They are then injected under great pressure to fill the cavity of a two-part mould. Diagram 47 shows a typical layout in which the granules are placed in a hopper and thence fall into a barrel in front of a plunger. The plunger moves them forward into the heated part of the barrel, heat being provided by band type heaters placed around the cylinder. To ensure that all the material is evenly heated, it is usual to incorporate in the barrel a streamlined piece of metal whose purpose is to spread the flow of plastics into contact with the hot face of the cylinder. This is known as a 'torpedo', and if it were not incorporated, it would be possible for the material in the

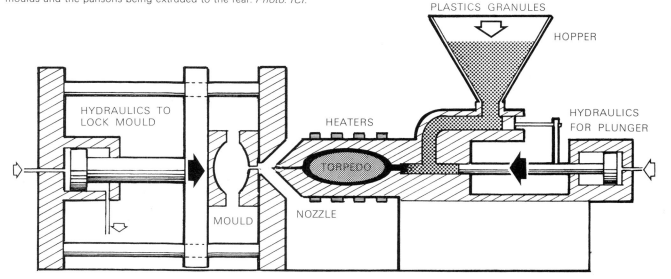

DIAGRAM 47. INJECTION MOULDING (modern machines may also be screw operated)

middle of the cylinder to be insufficiently heated. The molten plastics finally emerges from the nozzle and is injected under high pressure into the mould. In Diagram 47 the mould is shown in the open position.

The extremely high pressures produced at the interface of the mould are countered by a mould locking device — sometimes a simple hydraulic cylinder, sometimes an over centre elbow action which itself is hydraulically driven. These pressures may rise to 1500 tons. The mould is usually cooled to assist the hardening of the plastics and when the mould is split open the solid plastics impression can be removed. Mould temperature may be quite high, depending on the material being moulded. Temperature is usually a compromise between cold moulds and high production rates and hot moulds with slower production but producing better mouldings.' Removal of the moulding is usually assisted by ejector pins or metal bars which automatically push out the moulding as part of the mould opening operation. The quantity of material entering both the barrel and the mould is mechanically metered. Modern machines are commonly screw operated: in some cases, the screw is used both to carry the material forward by its rotating action, which is then stopped, and as a piston for the injection pressures.

Some plastics are more easily injection moulded than others: LD (low density) polythene, for example, flows at low temperatures and can be operated at low pressures; PVC (polyvinyl chloride), on the other hand, easily becomes degraded under the influence of heat and therefore can withstand only a limited 'dwell time' in the heating cycle. For a long time it was not possible to use thermosetting plastics for this process because of the obvious problems which might be caused by the material setting in the cylinder before reaching the mould, but modern machines have been adapted with accurate metering and control systems which allow all kinds of plastics to be moulded.

The mould The process is normally used only for extensive production runs; only through large quantity production can the high original cost of the mould be amortized. Moulds have to be rather massive and are usually made of steel to withstand the high impact and locking forces involved. The plastics flows from the nozzle of the injector into channels in the mould called runners, and these normally incorporate a constriction known as a gate, close to the moulding cavity. The plastics article when ejected is still attached to the material of the runner (known as the sprue) and the constriction caused by the gate forms a thin section which allows easy severance with minimum deformation.

Removing a test moulding in Rigidex (polythene) from a Windsor Autoplas injection moulding machine. *Photo: BP Chemicals (UK) Ltd.*

Fish kits by Streetly Man. Co. rotationally moulded in ICI's alkathene (polythene). *Photo: ICI Plastics Division.*

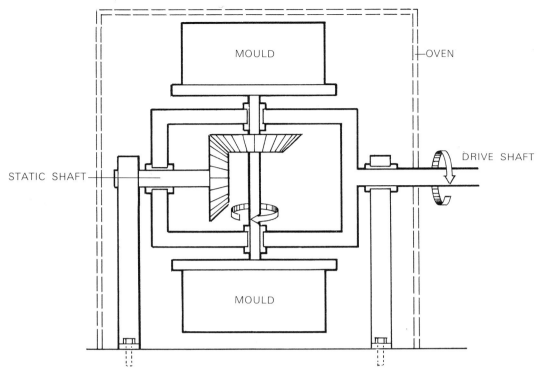

MOULD

OVEN

DRIVE SHAFT

STATIC SHAFT

MOULD

DIAGRAM 48. ROTATION MOULDING

ROTATION MOULDING (Diagram 48)

Rotation moulding is a sophisticated version of the slush moulding described in Chapter 8 and is used for such items as beach balls, large hollow storage tanks etc. Although more complex machinery is required, the basic process is simple. A closed mould, hollow on the inside, filled with a weighed amount of PVC paste, is placed on the spindle of a rotation moulding machine. This is a device which rotates one or more moulds about two axes set at right angles to each other. At the same time, the mould is heated — either by local heating or by operating it in an oven. By the peculiar action of the machine, the paste is distributed over the inside of the mould in a uniform thickness. After gelation, the mould is cooled and the article removed. It is possible to inject a quantity of polyurethane foam material so that the product is foam filled.

A typical industrial rotation moulder has a number of spindles, each carrying a mould, revolving about a central shaft. Cycle times vary from 12—20 minutes for small pieces to $\frac{3}{4}$ hour for very large pieces.

LAMINATES

Laminates may be built up from fibrous reinforcing materials impregnated with resin which are subjected to heating and pressure. The bulk of production takes the form of flat sheets, but a range of tubes, sections and rods is produced. All types can be machined. Decorative laminates incorporate a design which is pre-printed on paper. Usually a roll of decorated paper is unwound over rollers and passed through a bath of resin solution. The volatile solvent is evaporated and recovered in a heating chamber, and the material cut up into standard lengths for laminating. These are sandwiched between polished metal plates and subjected to heat and pressure. Laminates may also be made from thermoplastic sheets. Two colours may be laminated by heat and pressure providing a sheet on which patterns can be made by cutting through the top layer to the contrasting layer underneath.

IMPROVISING INDUSTRIAL MOULDING MACHINES
The following suggestions are included to assist those who wish to use industrial techniques for limited scale work.

Compression moulding Compression moulding has limited application beyond production work, but any press capable of sustaining pressures up to 5000lb./sq.in. can be adapted for the process providing there is an alternative means of heating the mould to between 150–200°C. Suitable band type heaters will be recommended by an element manufacturer if he is given all details (size, temperature, shape etc), of the mould it is required to heat. Circular section moulds are easily made up on a lathe and are best made in three parts — a cylinder, a base insert carrying the desired impression (this can be machined), and a plunger (see Diagram 49). The plunger and the base should be an excellent fit in the cylinder to prevent leakage. When the material flows, a sudden pressure drop will be noticed and, at this point, it is necessary to adjust and maintain adequate pressure.

'Lindiloo' portable plastics toilet cabin rotationally moulded in polythene. *Photo: ICI Plastics Division.*

Blow moulding See below, Injection moulding.

Injection moulding Injection moulders can hardly be improvised but very small bench or laboratory type models are available and older, manual production machines can be acquired at reasonable cost. The limiting factor in either case is the production of the mould (see 'Short Run Moulds'). Circular articles which can be lathe turned are relatively easy, but free forms are rather more difficult.

Rotation moulding A mechanically minded person should be able to improvise the rotation on two axes as in Diagram 48. The speed should be quite low, the action must be to tumble the powder inside the mould rather than to set up centrifugal effects.

IMPROVISED LAMINATES
The press Providing that a suitable press is available, laminates of limited area can be produced. Pressures up to 1000lb. per sq. in. are advised and these can be obtained on various types of press or from hydraulic vehicle jacks. If the maximum force of the press is known, the maximum area of the platens can be calculated.

The platens For small size laminates, these can be adapted

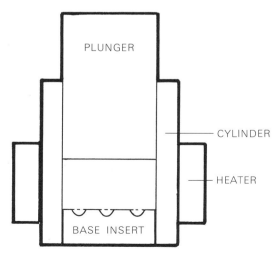

DIAGRAM 49. SIMPLE COMPRESSION MOULD

PLUNGER

CYLINDER

HEATER

BASE INSERT

from cast aluminium heaters (see Diagram 50). (If element manufacturers are provided with details of size, temperature to be attained, time to attain temperature and the supply available, they will recommend a suitable cast heater.) Alternatively they can be machined from aluminium plate and fitted with suitable cartridge heaters. Again element manufacturers will advise. In either case, it is necessary for the platens to be machined to an even thickness so that the pressure is distributed all over the faces. It is advisable to back up the aluminium platens with heavy steel plates.

Method The reinforcing material or sheet can be made from woven glass fibre, fabric or various papers. These can be pre-decorated. A system of impregnating them with resin must be devised: dipping and rolling out the excess is probably the most suitable.

The impregnated sheet is then gently heated, first to remove the solvents and then lightly to begin the curing of the resin. Material which has been part cured in this way is known as 'pre-preg'. A number of pre-pregs are inserted between stainless glazing sheets into the press and the requisite heat and pressure applied. Curing may take from five to fifteen minutes. On removal, the surface will match exactly the gloss of the plates. No doubt one or two trials will be necessary to get the optimum time/temperature/pressure ratio.

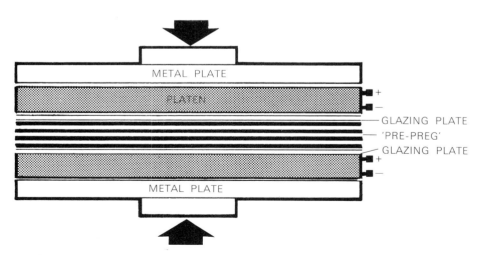

DIAGRAM 50. LAMINATING PLATENS

SHORT-RUN MOULDS

Steel is invariably used for moulds for mass production, but certain castable compounds can be employed for more modest runs or for proving prototypes and samples.

Castable 'Cement' for Blow Moulds The following recipe has been developed and proved by Messrs. Cascelloid of Leicester to whom grateful acknowledgment is made.

Ingredients: Magnesium oxide
Magnesium chloride (Hydrated $MgCl_2$ $6H_2O$)
Water
Silica flour

Method

1. Make up a 47 per cent w/w solution of magnesium chloride in water so that the specific gravity of the solution at room temperature is about 1.2.
2. Make up a 50/50 mixture by weight of the dry magnesium oxide and silica flour.

   To make the cement, mix the powder (2) with the solution (1) in the ratio of 9 parts by weight of powder (2) to 5 parts by weight of the solution (1) and stir well. Pour the mixture as for ordinary plaster.

Allow to stand overnight. The cement sets much more slowly than ordinary plaster. When set, full hardness can be achieved by drying overnight in an oven at 110°C. If oven drying is too rapid, stresses may be set up which cause the casting to shatter.

(This cement can develop a hardness on the Rockwell scale of 85 with a $\frac{1}{8}$'' ball and a 60 kg. load.)

Kirksite A Kirksite A, a pure form of zinc alloy, can be used to make cast moulds in metal. The 'as cast' finish which can be obtained with this material is quite excellent, but if highly polished surfaces are required, they can easily be worked up with hand tools.

When melted, the material is very fluid and reproduces surface textures accurately. It can be worked with hand tools which allows adaptations to the mould after it has been cast.

Data: Pouring temperature 427°C–454°C
(800°F–850°F)
Pattern allowance for shrinkage 1:96
(·1 mm. per cm. or ·125'' per foot)

Kirksite is regularly used for 'as cast' moulds for blow moulding, but when used for injection moulds, it is usual to incorporate it into a bolster. In either case, if cooling is required, it is a simple matter to fabricate and cast in cooling pipes.

Foundry procedures are simple; the alloy can be melted in an electric pot. The low pouring temperatures of such casting metals allow certain proprietary plasters to be used for direct metal casting of patterns and moulds.

Metal-casting plasters Herculite, Crystaperm and Hydrocal are suitable. They are specially formulated for metal casting applications and, apart from the gypsum base, contain refractory additives. Their mixing and handling is generally similar to normal casting plaster.

Adapting a bolster for injection moulds Diagrams 51a to 51c show a method of adapting a bolster for an injection mould to take a cast in-filling. The in-filling can be made of Kirksite or, in some cases, special resins.

CAUTION It is advised that cast injection moulds should not be made without a bolster because of the risk of bursting.

Resin tools The bolster described above can be used with resins which have been specially formulated to give strength at high temperature. Epoxy resins are favoured, but it must not be expected that resin moulds, when subjected to injection pressures and temperatures, will allow of anything but short runs. Best results are obtained using low melting plastics such as polystyrene. Because of the low thermal conductivity of epoxy resins, the moulding cycle will be much longer than for a metal mould. Epoxy resin manufacturers make limited claims for their materials in this connection and success cannot be guaranteed, but Devcon C or DB Toolform (High DT pouring grade) are favoured. In both cases, manufacturers' instructions should be followed and it is advised that moulds are oven cured.

In the main, about 2'' is the maximum depth which can be cast without risk of severe distortion due to exothermic action.

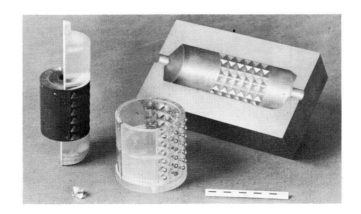

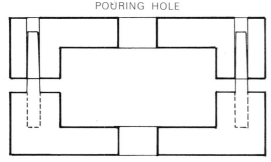

POURING HOLE

(a) BOLSTER MACHINED
TO RECEIVE EPOXY

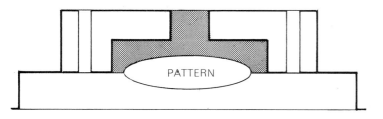

PATTERN

(b) PATTERN EMBEDDED TO
PARTING LINE AND ONE HALF
POURED

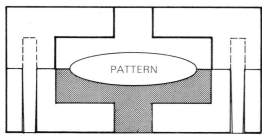

PATTERN

(c) BOLSTER INVERTED FOR
POURING SECOND HALF

DIAGRAM 51. CASTING AN INJECTION MOULD

Left: Zinc alloy cast mould showing stages in making the
prototype model. The centre section was cast in resin from the
Perspex assembly in the foreground. The neck and base portions
were turned in Perspex and attached to the resin casting. Made
by Emery Mould Castings, Welwyn Garden City.

As resins have a different coefficient of expansion from
the metal bolster, the system is not suitable for large moulds.
ICI have developed unstable compounds and techniques
for short run moulds, and can supply information.

PART 5
DATA

MATERIAL	RATIO BY WEIGHT	
	RESIN	METAL FILLER
Bronze	6–7	1
Iron ⎫ Lead ⎭	7	1
Brass	5–6	1
Copper	4–5	1
Aluminium	5	4

Note: Fillers take up approximately 50 per cent by volume, and resin quantities should be calculated accordingly.

INTERPRETATION OF MANUFACTURERS' DATA

Technical literature is produced by materials manufacturers who, in good faith, endeavour to give correct information concerning the properties of their materials, but as the performance of materials varies with such fundamental factors as time and temperature, it is difficult to give figures which hold good in all conditions.

The data which is published in this book, or in any other book for that matter, should be treated with caution by the novice and used as a guide only. For the purpose of selecting the most appropriate type of material, it will serve its purpose, but to be certain that a particular brand of material meets its requirements, it is best to test a sample in the identical conditions under which the article is to be produced.

PROPORTIONS FOR MIXING POLYESTER RESINS

WEIGHT OF RESIN	CATALYST OR ACCELERATOR			
	cc	4% oz.	cc	2% oz.
2 oz.	2	72 drops	1	36 drops
4 oz.	4	$\frac{1}{4}$ oz.	2	72 drops
8 oz.	9	$\frac{3}{8}$ oz.	4	$\frac{1}{6}$ oz.
$\frac{3}{4}$ lb.	$12\frac{1}{2}$	$\frac{1}{2}$ oz.	$6\frac{1}{2}$	$\frac{1}{4}$ oz.
1 lb.	18	$\frac{3}{4}$ oz.	9	$\frac{1}{3}$ oz.
2 lb.	36	$1\frac{1}{2}$ oz.	18	$\frac{2}{3}$ oz.
5 lb.	90	$3\frac{1}{4}$ oz.	45	$1\frac{1}{2}$ oz.
10 lb.	180	$6\frac{1}{2}$ oz.	90	$3\frac{1}{4}$ oz.

CHOPPED STRAND MAT
AVERAGE LAYERS REQUIRED

LENGTH	LAYERS REQUIRED
8'	4
10'	5
15'	6
20'	8

TABLE 1 PROCESSES BY WHICH MATERIALS ARE COMMONLY WORKED

	CAN BE PRINTED	VACUUM METALLIZED	ELECTROPLATED	THERMOFORMED	SPREAD	ROTATION MOULDED	BLOW MOULDED	COMPRESSION MOULDED	EXTRUSION	INJECTION	CASTING
POLYTHENE HD	✓	✓		✓		✓	✓		✓	✓	
POLYTHENE LD	✓	✓		✓		✓	✓		✓	✓	
PVC RIGID	✓			✓		✓	✓	✓	✓	✓	
PVC FLEXIBLE	✓				✓	✓			✓	✓	✓
POLYSTYRENE	✓	✓		✓			✓		✓	✓	
ACRYLIC	✓	✓		✓					✓	✓	✓
ABS	✓	✓	✓	✓			✓		✓	✓	
CELLULOSE ACETATE	✓	✓		✓			✓		✓	✓	
POLYPROPYLENE	✓	✓		✓			✓		✓	✓	
NYLON	✓	✓		✓			✓		✓	✓	
PTFE		✓						✓	✓		
ACETAL	✓	✓							✓	✓	
PF RESINS								✓	✓		✓
UF RESINS								✓			
POLYESTER								✓			✓
EPOXIDE			✓					✓			✓
POLYURETHANE											

TABLE 2 COMMON STOCK FORMS IN WHICH MATERIALS ARE AVAILABLE

	SHEET	ROD	TUBE	SECTIONS	MOULDING POWDER	LAMINATE	FOAM	LIQUID	FILM
POLYTHENE HD	✓	✓	✓	✓	✓		✓		✓
POLYTHENE LD	✓		✓	✓	✓		✓		✓
PVC RIGID	✓	✓	✓		✓				
PVC FLEXIBLE	✓		✓		✓		✓		✓
POLYSTYRENE	✓	✓			✓		✓		
ACRYLIC	✓	✓	✓	✓				✓	
ABS	✓				✓				
CELLULOSE ACETATE	✓	✓			✓		✓		✓
POLYPROPYLENE	✓	✓			✓		✓		✓
NYLON		✓			✓				✓
PTFE	✓	✓	✓						
ACETAL	✓	✓	✓		✓				
PF RESINS					✓	✓			
UF RESINS					✓	✓	✓		
POLYESTER						✓		✓	✓
EPOXIDE						✓		✓	
POLYURETHANE							✓	✓	

TABLE 3 SUITABLE METHODS OF WELDING

	FRICTION	HIGH FREQUENCY	HOT GAS	HEATED TOOL	SOLVENT	ULTRASONIC	IMPULSE (for film)	TEMP. (for heat sealing) °F
POLYTHENE HD	✓	Poor	✓	✓	X	✓	✓	250–375
POLYTHENE LD	✓	Poor	✓	✓	X	Poor	✓	
PVC RIGID	✓	✓	✓	✓	✓	✓	✓	
PVC FLEXIBLE	✓	✓	✓	✓	✓	X	✓	200–400
POLYSTYRENE	✓	Poor	Poor	✓	✓	✓	✓	220–300
ACRYLIC	✓	Poor	X	✓	✓	✓	X	
ABS	✓	X	✓	✓	✓	✓	X	
CELLULOSE ACETATE	✓	✓	X	✓	✓	X	X	400–500
POLYPROPYLENE	✓	X	✓	✓		✓	✓	
NYLON	✓	Good	X	✓	✓	✓	✓	
PTFE	X	X	X	X	X	X	X	
ACETAL	✓	X	X	✓	X	✓	X	
PF RESINS								
UF RESINS								
POLYESTER RESINS								
EPOXIDE RESINS								
POLYURETHANE								

NB Thermosetting materials cannot be welded.

TABLE 4 ADHESIVES AND ADHERENDS

ADHEREND	ADHESIVE TYPE
Metal	Epoxy, Acrylic Polyvinyl acetate Rubber based (natural or synthetic) Phenolics Polyurethane Polyamide
Wood	Urea formaldehyde Polyvinyl acetate Epoxy Cellulose acetate
Rubber	Epoxy Rubber based (natural) Phenolic Silicone
Acrylic (Perspex, Plexiglas)	Acrylic in solvent Epoxy Resorcinol formaldehyde Rubber based (synthetic)
Cellulose acetate	Cellulose acetate in solvent **Cellulose nitrate, Epoxy** Polyvinyl acetate Resorcinol formaldehyde
Nylon	Epoxy Phenolics Resorcinol formaldehyde
Polystyrene	Epoxy Polystyrene in solvent
Polythene and PTFE	Phenolics Silicone
PVC	Acrylics Neoprene rubber Phenolic-neoprene Phenolic-vinyl
Thermosetting (Epoxy, Melamine, Polyester, UF resins)	Epoxy Rubber based (synthetic) **Phenolic, Polyester** Resorcinol formaldehyde Urea formaldehyde

109

TABLE 5 ADHESIVE TYPES AND BRAND NAMES

ADHESIVE TYPE	BRAND NAMES (UK)	BRAND NAMES (USA)
Urea formaldehyde	Aerolite 308 (blue) Aerolite 308 (red) Cascamite Mouldrite Rawlbond	Aerobond Quick Stik
Resorcinol formaldehyde	Aerodux Cascophen	Eastman 910 Permabond
Polyvinyl acetate (PVA)	Evo-stik Resin W Polidene Bondfast Unibond Humbrol 22 Zoosamun	Vinylite UC1 UC2 Resgrip
Cellulose	Durofix Joy Stixin Le Pages clear Humbrol Balsa (66)	Duco Rez-n-glue
Epoxy	Araldite Twin pack Devcon Twinbond Bostik 7 Twin pack Evo-stik RDRA7033 Humbrol 88	Chemgrip Chemlok Easypoxy Adopox
Rubber based	Copydex Bondina Cow PA 33/64 (Nat.) Cow PA 69 (Syn.) Humbrol 99	Gripweld
Polystyrene in solvent	HMG Cement Le Pages polystyrene cement Styroglue Humbrol 77	Rez-n-bond MC25 Styfil
Acrylic in solvent	Tensol cements	Acrigrip Rez-n-bond MC25
Silicone rubber	Silcoset 151/152 Silastoseal B	Silastic Adrub-RTV
Phenolic	Cyanamid	Gripseal

TABLE 6 CHEMICAL RESISTANCE OF PLASTICS (20 °C)

	HIGHER ALCOHOLS	ALCOHOLS	ESTERS	AROMATICS	CHLORINATED HYDROCARBONS	KETONES	PARAFFINS	DILUTE ACIDS	CONC. ACIDS	DILUTE ALKALIS	STRONG ALKALIS	DETERGENTS	GREASE/OILS
POLYTHENE HD	G	G	F	F	F	E	E	E	G	E	E	E	E
POLYTHENE LD	G	G	F	P	P	F	F	E	G	E	E	F	G
PVC RIGID	E	E	F	F	F	F	G	E	E	E	E	E	E
PVC FLEXIBLE	F	F	F	F	P	F	F	E	E	G	G	F	E
POLYSTYRENE	F	F	P	P	P	F	G	G	G	E	E	G	G
ACRYLIC	Poor with crazing						G	E	F	E	E	E	E
ABS	E	E	F	F	F	F	E	E	P	E	E	E	G
CELLULOSE ACETATE	E	F	F	F	F	F	E	G	P	G	F	E	E
POLYPROPYLENE	E	E	F	P	P	G	F	E	G	E	E	E	E
NYLON	F to G. Some types affected.						G	G	P	G	G	G	E
PTFE	E	E	E	E	E	E	E	E	E	E	E	E	E
ACETAL	E	E	E	E	G	G	G	F	P	E	E	G	
PF RESINS	E	E	E	E	E	G	E	F	F	F	P	G	E
UF RESINS	E	E	E	E	E	E	E	F	P	F	P	E	E
POLYESTER	E	E	E	G	G	G	E	G	E—F	G	P	E	E
EPOXIDE	E	E	E	G	G	G	E	G	G	E	G	E	E
POLYURETHANE	E	E	E	E	F	F	E	G	P	G	G	E	E

E—Excellent, G—Good, F—Fair, P—Poor.
The degree of degradation varies
from complete dissolution to minor
softening, swelling or discoloration
and may vary with temperature.
ALWAYS TEST A SAMPLE.

TABLE 7 PROPERTIES OF PLASTICS

	ELONGATION WHEN STRETCHED (ASTM D 635)	SPECIFIC GRAVITY	MOULDING QUALITIES	SOFTENING POINT (VICAT)	MACHINING QUALITIES
POLYTHENE HD	50–500%	.96	Good	120–130°C	Excellent
POLYTHENE LD	100–600%	.91	Excellent	85–87°C	Moderate
PVC RIGID	2–40%	1.30	Fair	82°C	Excellent
PVC FLEXIBLE	——	1.30	Fair	——	——
POLYSTYRENE	1.0–2.0%	1.05	Good	80–100°C	Moderate to good
ACRYLIC	3–10%	1.20	Excellent	80–100°C	Excellent
ABS	350–600%	1.01	Good	85°C	Good to excellent
CELLULOSE ACETATE	6–70%	1.25	Excellent	70°C	Excellent
POLYPROPYLENE	50–500%	.91	Excellent	150°C	Excellent
NYLON	80–300%	1.13	Excellent	Melts 200–250°C	Excellent
PTFE	200–600%	2.10	Good but specialized	Melts 290–300°C	Excellent
ACETAL	15 Injection 75 Extrusion	1.43	Excellent	175°C	Excellent
PF RESINS	1.0–1.5%	1.30	Good with filler	——	Good with filler
UF RESINS	0.5–1.0%	1.50	Fair	——	Moderate
POLYESTER RESINS	——	1.20/2.06	——	——	——
EPOXIDE RESINS	5–10%	2.0	Good	——	Rigid good, flexible poor
POLYURETHANE	20–500%	1.15	——	150–185°C	——

TABLE 7 cont

	BURNING RATE (ASTM D 635)	TRANSPARENCY	EFFECT OF SUNLIGHT	ODOUR
POLYTHENE HD	Very slow	Translucent	Crazing and some degradation except when dark colours added	None
POLYTHENE LD	Very slow	Translucent to opaque		None
PVC RIGID	Self-ext.	Translucent to opaque	Slight discolouring	None
PVC FLEXIBLE	Self-ext.	Translucent to opaque		Some plasticizer odour
POLYSTYRENE	Slow	Transparent	Yellows badly	None
ACRYLIC	Slow	Very transparent	Virtually none	None
ABS	Slow	Translucent to opaque	May yellow	None
CELLULOSE ACETATE	Slow	Very transparent	Very slight	Slight
POLYPROPYLENE	Slow	Opaque	Some effect on all but dark filled cols.	None
NYLON	Self-ext.	Opaque	Discolours	None
PTFE	None	Translucent	None	None
ACETAL	Slow	Translucent	Slight discolouring	None
PF RESINS	Very low	Transparent to opaque	Darkening	None
UF RESINS	Self-ext.	Transparent to opaque	Darkening	None
POLYESTER RESINS	Very low	Transparent		None
EPOXIDE RESINS	Slow	Translucent	Yellows	None
POLYURETHANE	Slow	Translucent		None

TABLE 8 DENSITIES, SOFTENING POINTS, BURNING RATES OF EXPANDED PLASTICS

	DENSITIES (lb./ft^3)	SOFTENING POINT	BURNING RATE
EXPANDED POLYSTYRENE	0.75–4.0	90°C–110°C	Burns with drips. Made in self-extinguishing grades
EXPANDED POLYURETHANE	Rigid 2–20 Flexible 8–36	Rigid 100–150°C Flexible 50–100°C	Rigid: self-extinguishing. Flexible: burns. Flame retarded grade ignites less easily
PLASTICIZED PVC FOAM	1.8–8	150–180°C	Self-extinguishing
POLYTHENE FOAM	2–30	140–150°C	Burns very slowly dripping molten 'blobs'

TABLE 9 CHEMICAL RESISTANCE AND SOLVENT RESISTANCE OF EXPANDED FOAMED MATERIALS

	EXPANDED POLYSTYRENE	POLYURETHANE FOAM	PLASTICIZED PVC FOAM	POLYTHENE FOAM
CONCENTRATED ACIDS	When hot poor but can be good when cold	Poor	Hot poor, Cold good	Fair
DILUTE ACIDS	Excellent	Good	Good	Excellent
ALKALIS	Excellent	Good	Good	Excellent
ALCOHOL	Good	Excellent	Good	Excellent
KETONES	Dissolves	Poor	Poor	Excellent
AROMATIC HYDROCARBONS	Dissolves	Excellent	Poor	Excellent
CHLORINATED HYDROCARBONS	Dissolves	Poor	Poor	Excellent
DETERGENTS	Good	Excellent	Good	Excellent
GREASE/OIL	Poor	Excellent	Poor	Excellent

TABLE 10 SCALE OF IMPACT STRENGTH
(in descending order)

BEST	LDPE (low density polythene)
	PTFE (polytetrafluoroethylene)
	Nylon (wet)
	ABS (acrylonitrile butadiene styrene)
	HDPE (high density polythene)
	Nylon (dry)
	CAB (cellulose acetate butyrate)
	Rigid PVC
	Polypropylene
	Acrylic
WORST	Polystyrene

TABLE 11 RECIPES FOR DYEING PLASTICS
(data by courtesy of Messrs. Skilbeck Bros.)

	ACRYLIC	CELLULOSE ACETATE	POLYESTER	EXP. POLYSTYRENE
DISPERSOL OR DURANOL DYE	.5	.5	.05	.1
CALSOLENE OIL HS	3.0	3.0	3.0	3.0
BENZYL ALCOHOL	2.0	2.0	2.0	2.0
WARM WATER	94.5	94.5	95.0	95.0
DYEING TEMPERATURE	60–80°C	50°C	70–95°C	60°C
TIME (minutes)	15	10	10	5

NB   Dye bath should be stainless steel or vitreous enamel.

For paler or deeper shades, adjust time of immersion or concentration of dyestuff. Agitate when dyeing.

TABLE 12 PLASTICS MATERIALS SUPPLIERS

MATERIAL	TRADE NAME UK	MANUFACTURER	TRADE NAME USA	MANUFACTURER
POLYTHENE	Bexthene Alkathene Carlona Rigidex Iridon	BXL ICI Shell BP Commercial Plastics	Alathon Dow PE Tenite Catalin	Du Pont Dow Chem. Eastman Chem. Catalin
PVC	Cobex (rigid) Carina Darvic (rigid) Erinoid Velbex (flexible)	BXL Shell ICI Erinoid Ltd. BXL	Beutanol	Hartford
POLYSTYRENE	Bextrene Erinoid Carinex	BXL Erinoid Ltd. Shell	Styron Catalin Fostarene	Dow Chem. Catalin Corp. Foster Grant Co.
POLYSTYRENE (expanded)	Styrocell Bexfoam	Shell BXL	Styrofoam	Dow Chem.
ACRYLIC	Perspex Courtelle (fibre)	ICI Courtaulds	Plexiglas Lucite Orlon (fibre)	Rohm & Haas Du Pont Du Pont
ABS	Cycolac Vulkide A	Anchor Chem. Co. ICI	Cycolac	Marbon Chem.
CELLULOSICS	Cabulite (CAB) Bexoid Erinoid Celastoid	May & Baker BXL Erinoid Brit. Celanese	Tenite Celanese Lumarith	Eastman Chem. Celanese Corp. Celanese Corp.
POLYPROPYLENE	Propafilm Propathene Propylex Vulkide B	ICI ICI Brit. Celanese ICI		

TABLE 12 cont

MATERIAL	TRADE NAME UK	MANUFACTURER	TRADE NAME USA	MANUFACTURER
NYLON	Maranyl	ICI	Zytel Nylon	Du Pont Du Pont
PTFE	Teflon Fluon Polypenco	Du Pont ICI Polypenco	Teflon Fluoroplast Polypenco Halon	Du Pont US Gasket Co. The Polymer Corp. Allied Chem.
POLYESTERS	Melinex (film) Dacron (fibre) Terylene (fibre) Crystic (resin) Beetle (resin)	ICI Du Pont ICI Scott-Bader BIP	Mylar (film) Dacron (fibre) Gel Kote Hetron (resin) Plaskon (resin)	Du Pont Du Pont Glidden International Durez Allied Chem.
PF RESINS	Ciba Geigy Bakelite	CIBA Geigy BXL		
UF RESINS	Beetle	BIP		
MF RESINS	Formica (laminate)	De la Rue	Cymel	Cyanamid
EPOXIDES	Araldite	CIBA	Durax Epocast	Axel Plastics Furane Plastics
POLYURETHANE		Dunlop		

Addresses of Suppliers

Components for home-built equipment	UK	USA
Temperature indicating paints/crayons	Bayer Chemicals Ltd., 18/24 Paradise Road, Richmond, Surrey.	Tempil°, Hamilton Boulevard, 5 Plainfield, N.J. 07080.
Electric elements and heaters	Elmatic Ltd., Wentloog Road, Rumney, Cardiff CF3 8XH.	Progressive Service Co., 2720 Clark Avenue, St. Louis, MO 63103.
Toggle clamps De-Sta-Co	Insley Industrial Ltd. Eastern Road, Bracknell, Berks.	Dover Corporation, De-Sta-Co Division, Detroit, Michigan.
Toggle fasteners	Dzus Fasteners, Farnham Trading Estate, Farnham, Surrey.	Adjustable Clamp Co., 417 N. Ashland Avenue, Chicago, Illinois 60622.
	Camloc Industrial, 12 Hampton Court Parade, East Molesey, Surrey.	
Sunvic energy regulators	Satchwell Sunvic Ltd., P.O. Box 1, Harlow, Essex.	English Electric Corp., 500 Executive Boulevard, Elmsford, New York.
Marinite board	Marinite Ltd., Cape Universal House, Exchange Road, Watford, Herts.	Johns Manville International Corp., 22 East 40th Street, New York 10016.
General electrical equipment, transformers, ammeters, etc.	G. W. Smith Ltd., 27 Tottenham Court Road, London W.1., or 3 Lisle Street, London W.C.2.	Gloucester Eng. Co., 18 Sargent Street, Gloucester, Mass. 01930.

Pumps, pipe fittings for vacuum forming machines	Enots Ltd., Aston Brook Street, Birmingham 6.	Conair Inc., Franklin, PA 16323. Plasti-vac Inc., P.O. Box 5543, Charlotte, N.C. 28205.
Nickel chrome wire	British Driver Harris, Cheadle Heath, Stockport, Cheshire.	Olympia Tool Co., 3848 Park Avenue, Edison, N.J. 08817.
PTFE impregnated glass cloth	Fothergill & Harvey Ltd., Tygadure Division, Summit Littleborough, Lancs.	Eli Sandman Co., 280 Greenwood Street, Worcester, Mass. 01613.
Porous ceramic tiles	Doulton Industrial, Aerox Products, Filleybrooks, Stone, Staffs.	PPG Industries Inc., 1 Gateway Centre, Pittsburgh, PA 15222.
Thixotropic agents for plastisols, polyester resins, etc.	Aerosil, Bush Beech & Gent Ltd., Marlow House, Lloyds Avenue, London E.3.	Aerosil, Degussa Incorporated, 2 Pennsylvania Plaza, New York 10001.
Anti-static agents	G. H. Bloore Ltd., 480 Honeypot Lane, Stanmore, Middx.	Cadillac Plastic Co., Detroit, Mich. Axel Plastics Inc., Long Island City, NY.
Tensol cements	G. H. Bloore Ltd., 480 Honeypot Lane, Stanmore, Middx.	Imperial Adhesives Inc., 6315 Wiehe Road, Cincinnati, Ohio 45237.
Dyes for making plastics dyes (Dispersol, Duranol)	Skilbeck Brothers Ltd., 55–57 Glengall Road, London S.E.15.	Ferro Corp., Colour Div., 7050 Krick Road, Bedford, Ohio 44146.
Equipment and machinery	*UK*	*USA*
Hot air welding tools	Bielomatic, Cotswold Street, London S.E.27 0DP. Welwyn Tool Co. Ltd., Stonehills House, Welwyn Garden City, Herts.	Anchor Plastics Co., 36, 36 St., Long Island, NY 11106. Weldostron Corp., 907 Frelinghuysen Avenue, Newark 14, N.J.

Heat sealing equipment	Acru Tool Co., Ltd., Demmings Road, Cheadle, Cheshire.	Ames Bag & Packaging Co., 6006 S. Washington St., Marion, ALA 36756.
	Theco Electrical Ltd., 4–10 Wakefield Road, S. Tottenham, London N.15.	
Injection moulding machines	Small Power Machine Co., 368a Northolt Road, S. Harrow, Middx.	Jomar Industries Inc., 219, 33 St., Brigantine, N.J. 08203.
	Florin Ltd., 457–463 Caledonian Road, London N.7.	
Compression moulding machines	Fox & Offord Ltd., Aston, Birmingham B19 2RP	Clifton Hydraulic Press Co., 295 Alwood Road, Clifton, NJ 07015.
Vacuum forming machines	Parnall & Sons Ltd., Lodge Causeway, Fishponds, Bristol.	NRM Corporation, 47 W. Exchange Street, Akron, Ohio 44308.
Fluidized bed equipment	Plastic Coatings, (Machinery Division) Farnham Trading Estate, Farnham, Surrey.	Polymer Corporation, 2120 Fairmont Avenue, Reading, PA 19606.

General plastics materials	*UK*	*USA*
Polyester resins and general materials for glass fibre	Strand Glass Co., Brentway Trading Estate, Brentford, Middx.	Ashland Chemical Co., 8 E. Long Street, Columbus, Ohio 43216.
Acrylic, polystyrene, and materials for thermoforming	G. H. Bloore Ltd., 480 Honeypot Lane, Stanmore, Middx.	Amplast, 359 Canal Street, NYC 10013.
	Visijar Laboratories, Pegasus Road, Croydon Airport, CR9 4PR.	AIN Plastics Inc., 65 4th Avenue, NYC 10063.
	Griffin & George Ltd., Easling Road, Alperton, Middx.	Westlake Plastics Co., W. Lenni Road, Lenni, PA 19052.
PTFE	Polypenco Ltd., Gate House, Welwyn Garden City, Herts.	E.I. du Pont de Nemours & Co., Wilmington, DEL 19898.

Casting and mouldmaking materials	UK	USA
Temperature resistant resins for short run injection moulds etc.	DB Toolform, High D/T Pouring Grade, Hermetite Ltd., Tavistock Road, West Drayton, Middx.	Devcon C., Devcon Corporation, Danvers, Massachusetts.
Plasters suitable for hot metal direct casting	Herculite, Crystaperm, British Gypsum, Westfield, Singlewell Road, Gravesend, Kent.	Hydrocal, US Gypsum.
Kirksite alloy for cast moulds	Hoyt Metal Co. Ltd., Deodar Road, Putney, S.W.15.	National Lead Co., 111 Broadway, New York 10006.
Flexible moulding compounds	Vinamould, 19 West Street, Carshalton, Surrey. Silcoset, CIBA Geigy.	Vinamould, The Woodshed, 105, St. Mark's Place, New York 10001.

FURTHER INFORMATION

Much further information on plastics is available from various sources. As a starting point, the Plastics Institute's publication *Sources of Information on Plastics* may be consulted. It is available from:

> The Plastics Institute,
> 11 Hobart Place,
> London SW1W 0HL.

1. Attempt to cut thin sliver off edge of moulding

Powdery chips formed: thermo-setting resin

2. Hold lighted match to corner of moulding, smell the resultant vapour

Smell of phenol. Moulding usually brown or black
=
Phenol-formaldehyde

Fishy smell, moulding usually white or brightly coloured.

Urea-formaldehyde	**Melamine formaldehyde**

It is not easy to interpret between these two without laboratory tests

---

Fairly coherent sliver obtained indicates a thermoplastic. Confirm by applying a hot metallic rod to the moulding. Melting indicates a thermoplastic, although polyurethanes form a treacly mass

2. Drop the moulding a few inches onto a hard surface

Metallic noise indicates a styrene-containing polymer or polycarbonate (q.v.)

3. Burn a small piece of the moulding, blow out the flame and smell the resultant smoke

Smell of styrene only
=
Polystyrene or high styrene copolymer

Bitter smell as well as styrene smell; no smell of rubber
=
Styrene-acrylo-nitrile

Additional smell of rubber
=
ABS copolymer

A dull noise precludes polystyrene unless heavily loaded with butadiene

3. Place moulding in soapy water (or plain water if moulding is fairly large)

Moulding floats; polyethylene or polypropylene

4. Attempt to scratch moulding with the fingernails

High gloss moulding, does not scratch
=
Polypropylene

High gloss moulding, scratches to some degree
=
High density polyethylene

Sometimes less gloss on moulding, scratches fairly easily
=
Low density polyethylene

Moulding sinks; not polyolefin

4. Burn a small piece of the moulding, observe flame and ease of ignition

Burns with a yellow flame

5. Blow out flame, smell resultant vapour

Smell akin to methylated spirits
=
Polymethylmethacrylate (acrylic)

Smell of burning paper
=
Cellulose acetate or cellulose propionate (not distinguishable by simple tests)

Acidic plus smell of rancid butter
=
Cellulose acetate butyrate

Burns with difficulty.

5. Observe colour of flame while moulding is ignited

Greenish tinge to flame	Yellow flame	Little flame, material decomposes without charring, develops cellular structure before decomposition. Smell of phenol = **Polycarbonate**
6. Remove heat source, smell vapour	*6. Remove heat source, smell vapour*	
Acrid, sputtery, flexible moulding = **Plasticized PVC**	Distinctive smell akin to burning hair	
Slightly flexible moulding, acrid smell, no sputtering = **Vinylidene polymer**	*7. Press cold metal point to heated surface and then draw it away*	
Acrid vapour non-flexible, glossy moulding =	Threads form fairly easily = **Nylon**	

Rigid PVC or PVC-PVA copolymer

NOTE

Foamed or filled plastics are not considered in this table

Burns with difficulty with a blue flame. Blow out flame, smell vapour. Smell of formaldehyde
= **Polyacetal**

Acrid, also smell of burning rubber
=
Rubber-modified PVC

Acknowledgements

Without the unstinted assistance of friends in the
plastics industry, the preparation of this book would have
been an onerous task indeed. I am particularly indebted
to the staff of ICI, Shell and BXL and to those
companies for permission to quote from their
publications.
I would like specially to thank the following:
Mr. G. Born for his experiments with hot-wire cutters;
Mr. A. Geiringer for his assistance with heaters;
Mr. N. Woombs of Cascelloid for his assistance with
cast blow-moulds; Prof. Bailey of the University of Surrey,
Mr. A. Harness of ICI, and Antony Atha of Van Nostrand
Reinhold for advice and support.
Above all, I must acknowledge the debt I owe to the
staff and students of the West Surrey College of Art and
Design whose accumulated experience and research
provided the basis of so much of the text.
Finally, the book was not completed without some
neglect of domestic commitments and I am specially
grateful to my family for their forbearance.

Index

Glass fibre 72, *73, 74*, 75, 80, 82
glass reinforcing 72—9

Hardness 15
heat 13—14, 15, 26, 34—43, 88
heated tools 39, 47, *47*
heating mirrors 40
heat sealing 47—8

Ink 50, 52
insulation 15, 18, 24

Laminating 33, 101, 102—3, *103*

Metallizing 53
milling 28
molecular orientation 15, 17
monomer 11
moulding 15, 80, *81*, 104—5, blow
 moulding 97, *97*, 102, compression
 moulding 97, *97*, 102, *102*, injection
 moulding 99—100, *99*, 102, *105*,
 rotation moulding 101, *101*, 102, slush
 moulding 61, transfer moulding 97, *97*

Nylon 22, 62

Ovens 34
oven forming 36
overheating 26

Paraffin 10
Parks, Alexander 9
perspex 8, 15, 21
phenolics 22
pigments 13
plastics, properties 112—3
plasticizers 13
plastisols 53, 61
Plexiglas *see Perspex*
polyamides 16, 22
polyester resins 72—9, 80
polymer 11
polymerization 10
polyethylene 11, 16
polystyrene 9, 15, 21, 64, *64*, 69
polyurethanes 24
polyvinyl chloride *see PVC*
printing 50
PTFE 17, 62
PVC 9, 14, 18, 62

Reliefs 52
relief copying 82
routing 28

ABS 21
accelerator 72
acrylics 16, 21
adhesives 29, 33, 109, 110
alkyds 16, 23
aminos 16, 23
antioxidant 13

Bonding, chemical 10—11

Carbon 10, carbon black 15, carbon
 compound 10, carbon ring 10
casting 61, 69—70, 80—81
catalyst 13, 72
celluloid 9
cellulosics 16, 21
clamping 26—7, 90, 92, *92*
coating 62—3
colour 13, 15, 70
co-polymer 11
creep 15
cutting, hot wire 64—8, *65, 66, 67*

Dipping, cold 59—60, dipping, hot 54, 59
drilling 27
durability 15
dyeing 54, 116

Embedding 81—2
embossing 60
epoxides 16, 23, epoxy resins 16
expanded plastics 64—5, *64*
extrusion 96—7, *96*

Fibreglass *see glass fibre*
filament winding 82
filler 13, 75, 106
finishing 29
fluidizing 62—3, *62, 63*
foam 64, 80—1, polyurethane foam 69, *69,*
 81
forming, blow 37—9, *38, 39*, using clamp
 and template *36*, 36—7, oven 36

Sawing 28
screwing 28
shellac 9
solvents 13
spraying 60
spreading 60
stabilizers 13
stress 25

Tapping 2
thermal conductivity 47
thermoforming 34
thermoplastics 11, 13, 44
thermosetting 11, 13
thermosoftening 16
turning 28

Vacuum forming 87—95, *87, 89, 92*
vinyls 16,
vinyl acetate 11
vinyl chloride 11

Welding, friction 45—6, high-frequency
 48—9, hot air 44—5, ultrasonic 49